DATE DUE

Last Night in
Paradise

Also by Katie Roiphe

THE MORNING AFTER: SEX, FEAR,
AND FEMINISM

Last Night in Paradise
Sex and Morals at the Century's End

Katie Roiphe

LITTLE, BROWN AND COMPANY
Boston   New York   Toronto   London

First Edition

Library of Congress Cataloging-in-Publication Data

Roiphe, Katie.
Last night in paradise : sex and morals at the century's end /
Katie Roiphe. — 1st ed.
p.   cm.
ISBN 0-316-75439-0
1. Sex customs — United States.   2. Sexual ethics — United States.
3. AIDS (Disease) — Social aspects — United States.   4. Youth — United
States — Sexual behavior.   I. Title.
HQ18.U5R65   1997
306.7'097 — dc21   96-39508

10 9 8 7 6 5 4 3 2 1

HAD

Published simultaneously in Canada by Little, Brown & Company
(Canada) Limited

Printed in the United States of America

FOR

David Samuels

Contents

Last Night in
Paradise

Introduction

The summer after my junior year of college I was living in a dilapidated Victorian house in Cambridge, Massachusetts, with my boyfriend and some friends. I spent my days baby-sitting for a professor's two-year-old and my nights reading the biographies of poets next to a big window fan. The boys stayed up drinking until five or six in the morning and ate family-size boxes of Fruit Loops and Cocoa Pebbles. They had just graduated that June and were playing at adulthood, not all that successfully. We had long conversations about the rents in different cities. And then one day my parents called to say that my sister Emily had tested positive for HIV. Someone brought me a cup of tea. The sun shimmered through the leaves right outside my window. My father's voice was small and distant on the other end of the phone. I wanted to go home.

In the end I stayed. But for the rest of the summer I had a lot of trouble being where I was supposed to be. I rode my antique bike through the Cambridge streets in a state of such distraction I would go straight through traffic lights and cars would have to swerve around me. I would make plans to meet a friend for iced coffee in the Square and forget to show up. I would spend long afternoons in the air-conditioned libraries where I was supposed to be doing research for my senior thesis on Elizabeth Bishop. But when I looked up at the large, industrial clock, I would see that hours had gone by and I was still on the same page.

"You really are in outer space," my boyfriend would occasionally notice, and I was. My mind was occupied with questions that had no answers. They were questions about how my sister had become the person she was and how I had become the person I was, about how some people's mistakes come back to haunt them and other people manage to get off scot-free.

What had happened? I tried to look back into the slightly disorderly New York City brownstone in which I'd grown up — with cats and dogs curled up on the furniture, five sisters running up and down the stairs, parents who loved us — to find out what had gone wrong. Unlike almost everyone I know, I come from what was, on the whole, a pretty happy family. But amidst the warmth and noise, the cat hair and books, there was always a low-level tension surrounding everything that Emily did, which would sometimes burst into open conflict over dinner. Emily failing geometry. Emily kicked out of school. Emily banging her plate against the table and flying out of the room. As far back as I can remember, Emily seemed to have different ideas about life than my parents. And my parents seemed to have different expectations of her than of the rest of us. It was almost as if she were growing up in a different house, with different patterns and rules and routines. She'd sing to herself and sleep with the light on. She'd come home from school without her shoes. She'd tell us elaborate stories of what happened to her that turned out not to be true. I had a feeling that she was carrying some kind of danger inside herself like a bomb.

As we all got older, Emily became a sort of glamorous figure. She grew into her rebellion the way awkward children sometimes grow into their looks. I guess what really happened was that her rebellion organized itself into an aesthetic. It became tough and purposeful. She had dyed black hair, black nails, black lips, and earrings made from barbiturates dangling from her ears, and she seemed sleek and beautiful: the personification of all of the self-destructive impulses that accompany adolescence. When she went outside, her clothes seemed to taunt the neatly groomed ladies who passed by on Lexington Avenue in a cloud of pearls and Chanel No. 5. There was something upsetting about my sister's appearance even to my mother, who was not so neatly groomed, something calculated to provoke a worried look as Emily fished in my mother's purse for a twenty-dollar bill before dashing down the stairs and slamming the door. In the split seconds before Emily went out, the two of them would play out their largely unspoken drama of rebellion and reproach. And I would look up from my math homework, a kid in a white button-down blouse and a navy blue school uniform, and feel swelling in my chest an inexplicable pride in my wild sister.

Where did she go? What was she doing? She had the kind of sexiness that would, years later, be featured in magazines such as *Vogue* and *Harper's Bazaar:* wan, intense, and sleep deprived. She was funnier than anyone. She was one of those people who actually subscribe to the belief that all the world's a stage and everyone else in it a potential audience. As for men, she cast a sort of fast-talking spell on them and laughed her throaty, two-packs-of-Camels-a-day laugh, and they were completely under her sway. I pictured her perched on a barstool in some seedy bar captivating the male painters, sculptors, photographers, and poets of Avenue A. This was not, as it turned out, far from the truth. But there were other truths that were so far removed from the twenty-block radius in which I spent most of my life that I could not have imagined them even if I'd tried.

At one point Emily moved downtown to be closer to the world she was increasingly inhabiting. And one weekend morning my younger sister, Becky, and I went to visit her at her new apartment on Ninth Street and Avenue B. My mother dropped us off in the car, conveying to us, without actually saying anything, a certain amount of reluctance about letting us go. I can't remember anything about the visit itself, except that Emily was happy to see us, or the apartment, except that the door was broken and the hallway smelled of urine. When we got back out on the street, something felt wrong. It was too quiet for eleven-thirty in the morning. There were no children hanging around, no parents rushing out to get orange juice and doughnuts or walking dogs, as there would have been on Ninety-fifth Street at that hour. The neighborhood's inhabitants were all sleeping off whatever had happened the night before. The deserted block didn't feel safe. And when I saw the familiar brown Dodge Colt heading up the street, I remember wishing that we could take Emily back with us.

A photograph of my sister taken during this period shows a side of her I didn't quite perceive at the time. She is very thin, with porcelain white skin and glossy lips, and she stares at the camera with eyes heavily rimmed with kohl. She looks fragile and artificial, like a doll, like she is about to break. By that time it had gotten pretty bad.

Somewhere around the time that picture was taken, she moved back home. Her jokes stopped. Her sometimes infuriating desire to be the center of attention gave way to a kind of absence. She was living at home, but in some essential way she just wasn't *there*. The expression in her eyes was more effective than any "Do Not Disturb" sign. Becky and I tiptoed around her and talked quietly, afraid to arouse an irritation that we didn't quite understand. Why did everything seem to bother her? When I had friends over, they were scared of her fury at being woken up, her matted hair, her obvious state of distraction. There was no question of her being cool anymore. She had gone beyond cool into a kind of otherworldly detachment and decay: her face looked like it had not glimpsed the sun in years; her teeth were unbrushed, her clothes unwashed. She had gotten into a state that was impossible for even teenagers to romanticize.

She spent most of the day on a leather couch in the living room. This was my sister who once had swum so gracefully and tirelessly in a swimming pool that when she'd told me, age eight, she was half mermaid, I believed her. And now here she was lying on her side with a dead fish tattooed on her back. She barely moved at all. At first she watched television for hours, but later it seemed like whatever it was she was watching was inside herself. In the family we said that she was "depressed." There were bruises on her arms. There were nights when she didn't come home.

It got so that Becky and I rarely even referred to the unresponsive figure lying on the couch. We were busy worrying about whether boys were attracted to us or whether David B. was about to go out with Amy H. or whether Nick C. was ever going to call. We were worrying about really stupid things. And because of that, or because of some deliberate blindness on our part, it took us a surprisingly long time to figure out that our sister was a junkie. And even after we knew what was going on, we didn't tell our parents because of some unspoken code of adolescent loyalty that is now obscure to me.

The closest we ever came to seeing the drugs themselves, as opposed to hints or signs of them, was one night when we came home from a party and found Emily nodding. She was on the kitchen floor, her vinyl miniskirt hiked up around her hips, her head against the wall, an almost obscene look on her face. We stood there transfixed. Her skinny blond boyfriend with huge plastic glasses started chattering nervously trying to cover it up. It was the first time we'd ever heard him speak in more than a few guarded monosyllables. I felt bad for him. He repaired gargoyles on old buildings for a living, and with her eyes rolling into her head, crouched on the floor, my sister seemed for a minute like the most complicated gargoyle of them all.

Once she stole a painting right off my parents' living room wall. It was of a grim, bohemian-looking woman in a red beret by Raphael Soyer. Emily told Becky it was hers. "I'm just taking it back for a while," she called out cheerfully with the painting tucked under her arm. My father had begun collecting all the paintings and drawings on our walls, all the ships, Madonnas, and old ladies we grew up with, when he got out of the army in the forties. They were his only indulgence. Later that night, when my parents came home from wherever it was they were, they noticed the absence immediately. My otherwise gentle father reacted so loudly that we could hear the rich sounds of his rage all the way upstairs in our bedrooms. It was as if everything respectable and civilized about our family had vanished along with the woman in the red beret.

Eventually my parents went to the gallery where Emily had sold the painting and bought it back. The sallow woman was returned to her old spot on the wall, but the damage had been done. And for a long time after the incident was over, I remember feeling a sense of shame, as if something so awful had happened I couldn't tell my friends. It seemed like a sign, not just of my sister's desperation, but of a frightening level of disorganization: stealing something precious from your parents that they couldn't help but miss. I was worried.

During this same period, Becky and I were running around frantically trying to be normal teenagers like everyone else we knew. "You guys were *terrible*," Emily recently reminded me, and we were. We wore ripped jeans and hung out in Sheep Meadow in Central Park in the middle of the night, lying in the grass, smoking pot, looking at the stars, and avoiding the rats. We rode subways at night. We stopped speaking to our parents in full sentences. We slept with boys. We went to the Chinese restaurants that served unlimited free wine in big carafes to fifteen-year-olds and got smashed with our friends. We stood outside liquor stores in small groups until an amused passerby bought us bottles of very cheap, sweet champagne, and then we drank them together on stoops, by the fountain outside Lincoln Center, on the steps of the Museum of Natural History, or on the islands in the middle of Park Avenue.

Occasionally a policeman would come up to us and tell us that it was illegal to drink from open bottles on the street. Other than that, the city was ours. Everyone was game. No one ever had to be home. But I already knew something that many of my friends may not have known in quite the same way: freedom was not an unmixed blessing.

When I think back on those years, it seems like Becky and I might have been playing at being Emily. But in the end our attraction to danger was limited to the nights when we didn't have to study for tests or write papers. When the time came, we were going to take our SATs with number-two pencils like everyone else, then drive off to college in a car packed with lamps and towels. We were going to fulfill the destinies that our background and upbringing had prepared us for. We were conventional. We were never willing to take the kind of risks that Emily took. And some nights when she came home exhausted, smelling of Scotch and smoke, and peeled off her fishnet stockings, it would occur to me that I was never going to see as much of the world as she would. This may have seemed like a kind of cowardice at the time. And some days it seems like that now.

Eventually it all came out. Emily went to my parents and told them that she was addicted to heroin. They hadn't seen what was happening because the image of one of their children shooting up didn't register on their parental radar. It was too far removed from their own experience. Even though Emily's revelation created a new kind of turmoil, I remember feeling an overwhelming sense of relief. There were people to call. There were arrangements to be made. The atmosphere of secrecy and paralysis that had begun to take over our household gave way to action. My sister was going to a treatment center called Hazelden in Minnesota.

In some sense when Emily flew off to Hazelden it was like a warning to me and my younger sister, that everything warm and safe and middle class could slip away from you, that you could lose it all in the time it takes for a plane to leave the runway.

I am telling the story of what happened to my sister because of how tangled up in my mind it got with what happened to me, and because in some larger sense it is part of the story of a whole generation. Whose parents got divorced in the seventies, and whose siblings got too involved with drugs. Who grew up close enough to the sexual revolution to feel the heat of its promises, which involved having sex with as many people as you could and doing cocaine or pot or heroin or whatever drug you could get your hands on, without thinking about what might happen to you. But who also grew up seeing the consequences, or what were being presented as the consequences, of too much freedom. We watched the cautionary tales unfold in the papers one after another: an explosion of herpes cases, the emergence of a fatal sexually transmitted disease called AIDS, a "date-rape epidemic" on college campuses, Magic Johnson infected with the AIDS virus. We inherited some of the freedom of the sixties and seventies, but we also inherited along with it a sense of danger. In the back of my mind I have, like a photograph in a family album, an image of my sister crouched on the kitchen floor, her eyes rolling back into her head, which works as a kind of warning of how easy it is to go too far.

One day a letter from my sister, who was recovering in

Minnesota, arrived at my college dorm. When I read the first sentence, "I am a chemically dependent person . . . ," I started thinking about the very delicate line that separated her from most of the people I knew, half of whom seemed at the time pretty dependent on chemicals. One person I knew had toppled drunkenly off a fire escape; another had had to take Thorazine after a bad acid trip; another had smothered himself in a garbage bag inhaling nitrous oxide. Most of us didn't go to these extremes. But sooner or later almost everyone I knew found themselves drinking too much and waking up next to someone they regretted sleeping with. How was my sister different from the rest of us? Did she have a gene that made her take ordinary adolescent self-destruction just a little bit further? Most of my friends and I were just conforming to a college ethic that placed a premium on what I think, at the time, we would have called "experience." But it still felt to many people like something bad might happen if you lost control or stayed out too late or drank too much or went home with the wrong person. The game we were playing did not feel entirely safe.

"Where are you going?" my mother would ask my younger sister and me with an edge of anxiety in her voice, the unspoken end of her sentence being, *Don't do what your sister did.* Sometimes she would flash us a worried look if one of us opened the refrigerator and poured a second glass of white wine when we were home for a visit. It was as if we had inherited an extra measure of protectiveness like the hand-me-down winter coats we had worn as children. Isn't it possible to be *too* careful? I wanted to ask my mother, who didn't seem to think so. I developed a kind of heightened sensitivity to the warnings that were circulating through the headlines and talk shows: "Avoid drugs and alcohol." "Stay away from casual sexual encounters." "Stay in control." It was like seeing the pressure I felt to be careful, stable, and conventional echoed in the larger culture.

There is some part of me that is still the skinny ten-year-old who wants to follow her older sister into the subways underneath Manhattan and watches instead, with her face pressed up against the window, as the leather-jacketed form disappears into the night. There are still days when I wish I was more like Emily and could live without regard for the rules, and pick up and go to strange cities, do lots of drugs, get a tattoo, drink until I can't remember what happened the night before, and let out all my desires and longings and wildness regardless of the consequences. And then there are days when I want to marry the first lawyer I meet, push a stroller down Columbus Avenue, ride a stationary bicycle at the gym, and drink seltzer water at parties. I haven't entirely left behind the child who watches her parents worry, who feels a kind of tragedy in progress that she cannot stop or understand, and wants only, what so many of us now seem to want, to be safe.

Things change. Emily is living in Minnesota now. She's off drugs and alcohol, she's married to a man who exudes a sense of calm, and she writes poems, short stories, performance pieces, and movie reviews. She sends my parents a picture of her fluffy marmalade-colored cat, sitting on a patchwork quilt next to a Scrabble board, maybe as a way of showing them that her life has quieted down. And when she comes home this summer, I notice that her black hair has tiny streaks of gray in it.

At night we sit under the stars and talk about a miracle that has been in the tabloids lately: an autistic kid stayed alive for four whole days in a deadly swamp. Emily and I have become obsessed with this story. Something in the image of this little boy bobbing around with the alligators strikes us both as hilariously funny, and we can't stop laughing. My mother shouts down from her bedroom, "Quiet you guys," and my sister lights another cigarette, and we whisper to each other, and it's like being, for a moment, lifted out of time.

We don't talk much in my family about Emily being sick. But sometimes she has fevers. She disappears for long naps in the middle of the afternoon. A few months ago she published a darkly funny story about a woman with AIDS who takes out a personal ad because she can't find anyone who will have sex with her. She has also written a story for *The New Yorker*, which seems to be, among other things, about not being able to have children. I find these stories hard to read.

Emily's husband sits in the other room reading John Aubrey's *Brief Lives*, and we are looking at a copy of *Elle* and painting our fingernails. "God, look at her. She looks worse than I ever did," Emily says, pointing to an unhappy-looking jeans model in lurid blue eye shadow who looks like a fourteen-year-old girl about to turn a few tricks for a hit of something. And we study the girl's deep blue eyes for a minute as if we'll find there some hint about the past.

The screen door bangs shut. My parents have come home from a party, and my mother is still glowing from the gossip and energy of the crowd. One of her friends' daughters still doesn't have a boyfriend, and another one's son has become too stable and Park Avenue for his leftist parents. Another one's daughter has divorced the man she married only three months before, and another has gotten pregnant. Her words flow together into one long story about expectations and mistakes, confusions and rebellions, and how we do what we are supposed to do or we don't.

I find myself wishing for a happy ending, but there isn't one, just my sister and I sitting around painting our fingernails lavender, with the radio on, in a state of something like peace.

Last Night in Paradise

"Welcome to the post-pill paradise," says a suburban house-wife to her lover in John Updike's 1968 classic of sexual lib-eration, *Couples*, before she leads him upstairs to have sex on her king-size bed. And while it may not have been paradise exactly, there is a certain ease and carelessness to this woman's actions that gives the book a dated feel to anyone reading it now. If the late sixties bore any resemblance to paradise, it's not just because of the Pill; it's because of the larger faith in "sexual fulfillment," in doing what you want and not *think-ing* about it, which is precisely what we've lost over the past two decades and what gave the earlier period its rosy Edenic glow.

The lushness and promise of Updike's post-Pill paradise vanished into an atmosphere of anxiety and caution as her-pes, AIDS, date rape, and sexual harassment began hitting the headlines with an almost biblical persistence in the mid-eighties. Even the normally restrained *New York Times* Tues-day Science Section warned its respectable readers, in bold letters above an article about fruit flies, "THE PRICE OF

PROMISCUITY IS PREMATURE DEATH." The popular expectation that actions wouldn't have consequences, that you could do what you wanted, and that doing what you wanted was *healthy* had been transformed into a national obsession with consequences.

The most striking of these consequences is AIDS. From the beginning, the virus has lent itself to the kind of larger cultural interpretation that fascinates us: *What have we all done wrong?* Every age has its defining illness, the one that really makes its way into people's nightmares, the one that seems to tell us, with an eloquence beyond words, the story of our particular social decline. In previous times this eloquent microscopic symbolism has belonged to the plague, tuberculosis, cholera, and syphilis. In this case the AIDS virus appeared just in time to offer a vivid critique of the hedonism that we were already in the process of becoming disenchanted with. The startling appearance of a fatal sexually transmitted disease in the early eighties confirmed a deep puritanical conviction that much of America had secretly held for a long time: sexual freedom couldn't have been that simple after all.

Here was evidence that the sexual frolic of the past several decades had, in the bright Hollywood-influenced rhetoric of journalists and television broadcasters, a "hidden cost" and a "deadly toll." We suddenly found ourselves living in "the age of AIDS," or in France *"les années sidaïque,"* as if the disease itself characterized the state in which we were living. Aside from being a fatal virus that has taken the lives of nearly three hundred thousand Americans, AIDS has also diagnosed the general malaise of a culture bored and unsettled by its own excesses.

If the idea of a moral decline originated with the political right, with William Bennett, Ronald Reagan, and Newt Gingrich, it immediately impressed much of the country as being true. The point of view most commonly expressed by scholarly conservatives like Allan Bloom, who laments "parents' loss of control over their children's moral education at a time when no one else is seriously concerned with it," was echoed by regular guys like the HIV-infected boxer Tommy Morrison, who would say in his Rocky-inspired drawl, "There is a whole generation of kids out there like me who have totally disregarded our moral values."

The increasingly common perception that the country was in some sort of moral crisis colored the early reports of the AIDS virus as reporters, journalists, and television broadcasters mused about the "cost of the sexual revolution" and the "price of sexual freedom." The historical accident of the virus inspired all sorts of people to comment on the need for "commitment," "monogamy," "stability," and "trust" and on the general absence of moral principle. Kevin Johnson, the point guard for the Phoenix Suns, would reflect on *This Week With David Brinkley,* "We've got to return to traditional values." The *New York Times* reported, "Caution is in. The one-night stand is on the way out," and part of what was broadly being considered "caution" was in fact a return to the values of a previous era. After the breakdown of tradition in the sixties and seventies, a new morality rose out of the fears of the epidemic — a morality with its own jingles, posters, movie plots, public service ads, bureaucratic edicts, and cultural pieties; its own parables about the perils of promiscuity involving athletes and nice girls who get AIDS.

In magazines, newspapers, and talk shows, the most common scenario of infection would involve falling into bed with someone you don't know that well and waking up the next morning with the disease. These are stories that many, if not most, of us can easily imagine ourselves taking part in. Their drama lies in their closeness, their plausibility. "It's absolutely the worst way in the world to die," a girl from the University of Wisconsin tells a reporter from *Rolling Stone,* and it's certainly the way we as a culture, obsessed as we are with sex and its dangers, think most about dying.

"Jesus Christ, I remember exactly where I was," a slim Hispanic boy in a faded red baseball hat and an earring tells me. "I was home sick that day, bored. I turned on the television and there it was." He is talking about the news of Magic Johnson being infected with the AIDS virus. "Man, it really hit me," he says, and it occurs to me that this seventeen-year-old is describing the exact moment he heard about Magic Johnson with the same tone of gravity and precision, the sense of history colliding with his own life, that a previous generation uses when they talk about where they were when John F. Kennedy was shot. As the pale blue light of the newscast flowed into his living room, it took on the same depressing aspect as living rooms in 1963: in that one highly emotional televised moment, his world changed.

High school has always involved a certain amount of theater. But for this new generation of boys and girls in Stussy baseball hats, the drama is intensified by the presence of a deadly disease that they are constantly being told they might get — by teachers lecturing about condoms in classrooms, public service announcements blaring warnings from the radio, and experts chatting about the danger of "teen sex" on television. At a bus stop you can see the irony of the times acted out in a kind of tableau: a fifteen-year-old making out passionately with his girlfriend in front of a giant Benetton ad brightly displaying a man's chest stamped with the words "HIV positive." It's like being, for a moment, inside their minds.

By the time these kids began thinking about sex, the fatal virus had already become part of the buying and selling of colorful sweaters and scarves, part of business as usual. The fact that some people die from sex is a thought that teenagers are used to. Ask anyone under twenty when she first learned about AIDS, and she will say she always knew about it. Consider for a moment a bunch of girls from Stuyvesant High School in New York sitting in the living room of one of their houses, feet up on the glass table, fashionably ratty knapsacks thrown on the floor, a single piece of pizza on a greasy paper plate passed between them.

"There's all of this shit going on," begins a plump girl with an angelic face, sparkling blue eyes, and wispy blondish hair falling from her ponytail. "My friend Mary knows this woman who was on an airplane. I don't remember where she was going. California, maybe. She met this really handsome guy, and they hung out all night and went to a fancy hotel. They slept together. Unprotected." She stops to make sure everyone caught that. "The next morning he gave her a present and told her to open it later. On the airplane home she took off the ribbon and unwrapped the box. Inside was a tiny black coffin, and inside the coffin was a note saying, 'Have fun, you have AIDS.'"

"Wait," says a pretty black girl sitting cross-legged on the couch. "I've heard this story before."

"The way I heard it," says a tiny girl with painted black fingernails taking a big stretchy bite of pizza, "it happened to somebody's aunt."

I've also heard this story before. It's one of those archetypal horror stories that get passed around, changing slightly with each telling but remaining in basic structure and moral essence the same. It circulates through networks of teenagers around the country in countless living rooms over countless pieces of pizza. I've heard so many versions of it, in places as far apart as Tennessee, New Jersey, and Washington State, that it gives me the illusion of small-town familiarity, like finding a black leather-bound Gideons' Bible in the drawer of a hotel room no matter where you are. The action always takes place at one remove. It always happens to a friend of a friend. Sometimes the story goes like this: A man meets a beautiful woman at a bar — or a party, a museum, an airplane — and they spend the night together. The next morning he wakes up, sun streaming in, sheets crumpled next to him, and she is gone. Scrawled across the mirror in bright red lipstick are the words "Welcome to the world of AIDS."

These are not, in the strictest sense, stories about the AIDS virus. In fact the exact same stories circulated at the beginning of the eighties with the punch line "Welcome to the world of herpes," the medical details being basically interchangeable and beside the point. What we're really hearing are steely moral parables on an increasingly popular theme: the dawning conviction, after the brief utopian interlude of the sixties and seventies, that sex has consequences after all. You can't just do whatever you want. You can't indulge every desire and expect to get away with it. The punch line "Welcome to the world of AIDS" is often delivered by an apple-cheeked tenth-grader with a brisk, puritan satisfaction that occasionally borders on glee. And in the excited tone of her voice ("Just *look* what happens if you behave irresponsibly"), you can hear the swift formation of a new sexual ethos. The ravishing stranger sitting next to you at the bar, all frosty pink lipstick and plunging neckline, object of fantasy circa 1969, has grown violent and sinister. Her bedroom eyes are not just promising bedrooms anymore.

Sitting with their feet up on the coffee table, the Stuyvesant girls move on to a more specific kind of gossip. "So he said, 'We just did it right there in the grass,' " recounts a pretty girl in black. "So I said, 'Wait a minute, Ben, are you telling me you are having unsafe sex?' So he said, 'Yeah.' I was totally shocked." Her eyes glitter dangerously.

"You know, condoms break. We are never really safe," she continues with an air of great determination. "When I am eighty years old, I want to be able to look back and say that I have never had unprotected sex."

"You can't be too careful," pipes in one of her friends, wearing the latest in teenage schizophrenic chic, greasy hair parted down the middle, and layers of mismatched shirts in festive stripes. "You never know who's clean."

Although they keep lapsing into official blackboard phrases, these girls are not just parroting what they learned in health class or read in *Sassy* magazine. Their tones are electric, jammed with an energy and zeal that is all their own. You can feel the fast sequence of images beneath their conversation as each one pictures herself beneath satin sheets, heroically whispering "not without protection" into some scruffy boy's ear, or asking for a twelve-pack of condoms from the handsome guy behind the counter at Love's or CVS, dissolving into giggles, the thrill and danger merging. They are almost buoyant.

"No orgasm is worth risking your whole life for," says the striped girl passionately.

It's as if there has been a chemical reaction between the received ideas — "You can't be too careful" — from parents, teachers, posters, magazines, talk shows, the six o'clock news, and their own deepest, most private feelings. The danger is personal. The crisis is real. Of course the drama of the AIDS virus appeals to the turbulent, lyrical extremes of the adolescent imagination: if you have sex, you might die. Everything becomes just the way teenagers like it, *serious.* The idea of a fatal sexually transmitted disease makes perfect sense in a world where everything is amplified, where doors slam, tears flow at the dinner table, political opinions are absolute, and phone calls are urgent, five hours long, and take place in the middle of the night.

The strange fervor "safe sex" produces, however, is not confined to teenagers. Over the past ten years the worry about AIDS has taken on a life of its own. After pages on how to wear the new pastels and "Loser Guys: How to Spot Them," *Mademoiselle* gives its young readers chirpy advice on condom etiquette: ask him at the moment of truth, "May I show you something in the rubber motif?" Other women's magazines offer helpful hints on how to make safe sex *fun* and identifying the best place to buy "itsy-bitsy finger condoms" so that you don't even have to *touch* dangerous body parts.

The first condom store in the country, Condomania, with addresses on Bleecker Street in New York and Melrose Avenue in Los Angeles, opened in 1991 on the same principle, its dazzling shelves laden with glass candy jars filled with blue, purple, yellow, ribbed, and glow-in-the-dark condoms. They also carry mint-, chocolate-, strawberry-, and passion fruit–flavored condoms, condoms in the shape of coins or lollipops, and sleek, state-of-the-art ultrathin condoms from Japan. "Our philosophy is to present condoms in a fun, nonthreatening way," Adam Glickman, the twenty-nine-year-old creator of the chain, explains. "We're the Walt Disney of safer sex."

This is not just our American flair for advertising and sloganeering and sighting the consumer potential in a crisis. It's not just rising to the occasion or making the best of a bad situation. There is a kind of breathlessness to "itsy-bitsy finger condoms" or "May I show you something in the rubber motif?" or "No orgasm is worth risking your whole life for," an eagerness, a peppiness, a joy taken in the discussion and controlling of risk, that goes beyond the call of duty. "One in five heterosexuals could be dead from AIDS at the end of the next three years," Oprah Winfrey told millions of Americans one afternoon in 1987, also going beyond the call of duty with a wild inflation of the numbers. "Now No One Is Safe from AIDS," declared the cover of *Life* magazine that same year. "The virus is running rampant through the heterosexual community," warned the renowned sex experts Masters and Johnson. Altogether, sexual fear was being marketed with a zealousness that cannot be explained away by the need to spread the word. America seemed, at times, to be embracing the AIDS epidemic — not the terrible disease itself, but, in its abstract form, the *idea* of sexual peril. It had inspired a perverse enthusiasm. The ardor lay in the discovery of a real and visible danger — an actual crisis to give form and meaning to our free-floating doubts and anxieties about sexual freedom.

The change in sexual morality was, of course, astonishingly quick, and the quickness itself is part of what continues to confuse us. In a Gallup poll in 1969, 80 percent of Americans thought premarital sex was "wrong," by 1973 almost half the country thought it was acceptable, and by 1975, at least among younger people, the number had risen to three-quarters. And these were, after all, not just abstract attitudes casually checked off on a questionnaire. These were actual changes that could be measured out in bedrooms, hearts, tears, diary entries, novels, Pill prescriptions, and psychiatrist bills. Divorce rates skyrocketed; guilt plummeted. As Allan Bloom put it in *The Closing of the American Mind,* "The kind of cohabitations that were dangerous in the Twenties, risqué and bohemian in the Thirties and Forties, became as normal as membership in the Girl Scouts."

I myself witnessed this exhilarating and tumultuous period from the distant, disapproving, order-craving vantage point of childhood. One of my older sisters, who was then in college, told me that she had slept with fifty men. "*Fifty* men?" I asked, incredulous. To which she answered, after a moment of thought, in a bored tone, "Those are just the ones I can remember."

But nonchalance didn't last as a national attitude. "All of

this fucking, everybody fucking, I don't know, it just makes me too sad. It's what makes everything so hard to run," observed a tired Rabbit Angstrom at the end of John Updike's saga of sixties chaos, *Rabbit Redux*. Scattered across the country, there seemed to be countless other Rabbits, sitting in their middle-class suburban houses, wives having run off and come back, engaging in the same sort of epiphany: enough is enough. The heady atmosphere of promiscuity began to get complicated, and the strange, touching faith that sex would somehow increase the sum total of human happiness began to fade. The couples who wrote optimistic, bestselling guides to "open marriage" began to break up, and the disillusioned consumers of these guides began to search for new moral codes, a search that would eventually take on an almost religious intensity and comprehensiveness.

The American craze for regulation and instruction extended to such intimate matters that by the early nineties, classrooms, restaurants, cars, and offices were, at least theoretically, transformed by new rules about smoking, seat belts, whom it was appropriate to ask out on a date, and what kind of jokes you were allowed to make to someone in a less powerful position. There was an odd literalness to the pursuit, a fondness for things written down, for memos, posters, codes, and guidelines. It was not entirely unheard-of, during this period, to walk into the bathroom of a bank or insurance agency or television station and find posted on the door an official list of what was and wasn't acceptable to say in the office: "Do not comment on a colleague's personal appearance." It was as if the dangerous sexual force that had been unloosed in the sixties, the chaos and uncertainty of it, could be controlled by clarity and exactitude.

Universities, which had been hothouses of sexual freedom in the seventies, became in the nineties the central location of sexual fear. The sense of overwhelming freedom that had once electrified campuses with sexual frisson now sparked serious discussions and workshops about date rape and sexual harassment in student centers and freshman dorms across the country. The fear that seemed to hover over parties and dorm rooms and campuses late at night, and the confusion of waking up in a strange bed next to someone you didn't know, had been thoroughly politicized. The fear had been parcelled out into "issues." It was not surprising, then, that the general pursuit of etiquette would culminate in 1993 at Antioch University, a small liberal arts college in Ohio, with the absurd and much-publicized creation of a code of conduct requiring "verbal consent" at every stage of every sexual act: "Consent must be obtained verbally if there is to be any sexual conduct or contact; if the level of sexual intimacy increases during an interaction (i.e. if two people move from kissing fully clothed, which is one level, to undressing for direct physical contact, which is another level) the people involved need to express their clear verbal consent before moving to that level."

During the somewhat surrealistic period when this code was being taken seriously on the front pages of the *New York Times* and commented on in newspapers and magazines all over the world, I was giving talks about feminism and the political perils of going back to a Victorian ethos on college campuses. Wherever I went, there was inevitably some sweet-faced eighteen-year-old boy who would raise his hand and ask, in a tone so pressing it banished any political concerns, "But what *are* the new rules? How *should* we act when we're out on a date?"

These eighteen-year-olds were asking out loud a question that most of us who have reached a more cynical age still have lingering somewhere in our hearts, the question implied by all the new codes about sexual harassment and "verbal consent" and the bestselling book *The Rules,* and that is, *Where are we supposed to stop?* All the voices that we hear from movies, books, magazines, advertisements, pop songs, and friends merge into a tolerant and optimistic buzz: there is nothing wrong with sex before marriage; go out, have a good time, have sex with people you don't love, follow your heart, fulfill your desires; there is nothing to stop you but the limits of your own appetites. During the May 1968 student revolution in Paris, posters plastered all over the city read, "It Is Forbidden to Forbid." And in America in the seventies and early eighties, it was still pretty much forbidden to forbid. There was practically nothing, at least as far as normal sexual practices were concerned, that was actually considered *wrong.* And as the explosion of codes of conduct and rules about sexual harassment in the mid-eighties would reveal, all the indulgent voices left some fundamental need for control unsatisfied.

Janet Malcolm writes that "the nineteenth century came to an end in America only in the 1960s," and the truth is that as we approach the next century, the previous one seems to be exerting more and more of an imaginative hold on us. It appears to us in the soft, enchanting colors of an impressionist painting: the corseted ladies trotting on horses, the chaperoned strolls along the seaside, the sheer formality of existence, the ease and rightness of it all. The progressive whirl of the past few decades, the lifting of one taboo after another, the speed of political change and the resulting freedoms, seem to have left us with a deep, almost perverse nostalgia for the most stifling, moralistic moment in history we can imagine.

Only it doesn't seem stifling and moralistic anymore; it seems *civilized.* We long to reproduce the neatly trimmed rose gardens of Jane Austen's England — the lowered glances, flirtations, innuendos, and felicitous simplicities of the nineteenth-century marriage plot. The recent surge of interest in Austen — the most obvious manifestation of which is the unlikely translation of her quiet courtship novels (*Sense and Sensibility, Persuasion,* and *Emma*) into Hollywood Technicolor — provides a kind of literal expression of this impulse. And in darkened movie theaters across the country, audiences avidly consume the rich fantasies of ringlets and reticence. This fascination with Austen is not just about style; it's about the sensibility that's been lost. But what is its appeal? I know, at least for myself, what I find so reassuring about the Emmas and Annes and Elinors gliding modestly across the screen is the startling neatness and security of their destinies. They fall in love with the man whom history and class and tradition have chosen them for. These movies are cleverly marketed to a jaded audience straining to hear, as we listen to the nineteenth century, in Dolby sound, piped into the twentieth, the gentle voice of social persuasion saying, *This is the way it's supposed to be.*

The contemporary American version of Jane Austen's marriage plot — or that of the 1950s, for that matter — is hopelessly complicated. The romantic stories currently buzzing through our phone lines have no clear progression or obvious endings. Relationships come together and dissolve in a general atmosphere of haziness and impermanence. People live together and move out. They sleep together for indefinite periods. They marry later. They travel light. I recently overheard a pretty woman at a party say, not without regret, "When our mothers were our age, they had husbands instead of cats." She is one of the many normal, pulled-together people I know inhabiting the prolonged, perplexing strip of adolescence currently provided by this country to its twenty- to thirty-year-olds. The romantic sensibility — cats or husbands? — is fragile and confused. We go to parties and occasionally fall into bed with people we don't know well, but we also have well-read paperbacks of Austen's *Mansfield Park* or *Emma* lying open on our night tables: the dream of a more orderly world.

The actual site of all this ambivalence was located, for me, in a tiny, cluttered bathroom I shared with three women in college. Every Saturday and Sunday morning there would be a different man, belonging to one or the other of us, brushing his teeth, with a fluffy pink towel wrapped around his waist. At first the rest of us would glance at him curiously through the sliver of the open door or as he emerged, freshly showered, into the ashtray-scented air of our common room. But as the months wore on, we stopped even seeing those endless repeating men in towels. There didn't seem to be anything wrong with what we were doing. We were simply following, night after casual night, the first principle of contemporary American life: entertain yourself.

I remember one spring morning waking up early, leafing through the paper, idly glancing up at one of the toweled men as he left the bathroom and disappeared into one of the bedrooms, and somehow in that moment everything changed. I recognized the pale, skinny chest from a few weeks before. That time he had disappeared into a different bedroom. All of a sudden I felt almost sick with the accumulated anonymity of it, the haphazardness, the months and months of toweled men. That morning I felt, for the first time, the general fatigue that was soon to be captured in the "safe sex" jingle "You are sleeping with everyone your partner has ever slept with"; the true anxiety of the crowd; the uneasy sensation that there were simply too many of us drifting in and out of each standard-size, metal-frame, dorm-room bed. It was then that I first felt a hint of our absolute readiness for limits, for someone to say, for whatever reason, this is not a healthy way to live.

It was out of this general mood of exhaustion that the emerging philosophy of "safe sex" would take its most compelling images. The nightmarish echoes that would soon become the basis for countless public service announcements about safe sex — "You've had sex with two people, and they've each had sex with two people, and each of them has had sex with two people" — aptly described the world as I experienced it that morning: the endless procession of half-naked bodies parading through the dusty sunlight of our common room. I would soon see my private panic, and that of countless other people in other dorm rooms, projected across the billboards and television screens of the larger culture as the message of "safe sex" fused completely and inextricably with the uneasiness that was already there.

If our anxiety about disease sends us to test centers and gives us nightmares, what it *doesn't* seem to do is change our behavior in any straightforward way. The standard magazine version of events is that there has been, over the past ten years, a "move-ment toward monogamy" and a "movement away from casual sex." But the word "movement" itself implies a kind of or-derly, sensible retreat from promiscuity that doesn't convey the weirder, more haphazard aspects of our behavior. The truth is that the fear of disease incorporates itself into our lives in irra-tional, almost arbitrary ways: We wait five weeks after know-ing someone before sleeping with him, or we wait three days. We wait until he buys us dinner, or we wait until we've both been tested. We use condoms with people we meet at parties, but we don't use condoms with people we knew from school. We buy twelve-packs of condoms and tuck them in the back of a drawer, but we don't actually use them; or we get an AIDS test every few years, but we don't bother to use condoms in between. Everyone I know has his or her own system. None of them makes much sense.

The content of the rules we invent for ourselves is not par-ticularly scientific, but that may be because it's not the content that matters. Now that most of us no longer believe that sex before marriage leads to the flames of hell, now that sexual ex-pression is considered "normal" and "healthy" and *not* having sex before marriage is, if anything, considered a bit peculiar, AIDS has offered us a biologically compelling alternative to old-fashioned morality. It's not that sex is wrong; it's that it's not *safe*. Gratefully we have met the real peril of sexual dis-ease with the real need for rules, even if we're not going to fol-low them, for some kind of structure to replace the moral and religious structures that we've lost.

Recently I came across an old journal from when I was fif-teen that summoned up the bright, sensual landscape of a lost world. My friends and I were beginning to go to hotel bars and flirt with businessmen over whiskey sours and little bowls of Pepperidge Farm Goldfish; we were beginning to have the long, complicated phone calls with boys that we called "relationships." The more poised and precocious among us were beginning to go out with our English teachers to learn, along with the themes of *To the Lighthouse,* how to give blow jobs. It was amidst this general climate of sexual experimentation that I confessed into the ivory pages of my journal what I would never have confessed to my flamboyant friends: "the horrible, embarrassing truth is that I'm actually afraid to have sex." It seems to me now, reading the humiliated scrawl of my former self, that fear is not an entirely outlandish feeling for a fifteen-year-old to have toward sex, even before the threat of AIDS made everything more complicated.

In the absolute terror of the disease, the slim possibility of getting it through heterosexual sex, the less than 1 percent chance that a condom could break, we have found a certain clarity. In a culture where fifteen-year-olds deciding not to sleep around is newsworthy enough to hit the cover of *Newsweek* ("Virgin Cool," October 14, 1994), the fear of the virus promises an escape from the exhausting and uncompromising ideals of hedonism. It offers us limits in a limitless world.

No one knows exactly what the risk is. It's shimmering and chimeric; something we believe strongly in but can't see. We tell each other that it's "out there." Giant eighty-foot condoms fly, like strange hallucinations, above football stadiums as part of the ambitious new advertising campaign for Sheik condoms, reminding us of the danger. It enters intimately into our

lives. But amidst the flood of warnings, the countless magazine articles on "the New Dating Game," the classroom lectures on "safe sex," we still don't know the proportions of the
risk. "AIDS MAY DWARF THE PLAGUE" ran a dramatic *New
York Times* headline in 1987, quoting Dr. Otis R. Bowen, then
secretary of health and human services. But that same year, as
Susan Sontag pointed out, Bowen said, "This is not a massive,
widely spreading epidemic among heterosexuals as so many
people fear." Over the years we would read in *Glamour* that
"statistically the risk to heterosexuals is low" and in *Newsweek*
that heterosexuals were "the volcanic underside of the AIDS
epidemic." We would read that the virus was spreading rapidly into "the general population" and that it wasn't. And in
the ambiguity — the mysterious margin of error contained in
the phrase "safer sex," the curious absence of statistics telling us exactly what our chances are of getting AIDS through
heterosexual sex — we would see what we chose to see. The
abstinence activist would see one thing. The terrified fifteen-
year-old virgin would see another. The risk itself became a kind
of blank canvas against which we could project our own mental
states and cultural needs.

The dramatic world that has been presented to us for so long
in advertisements, television specials, billboards, and classrooms, in brilliant colors and MTV graphics, is a world of
absolute and immediate peril. It's a world of tearful mothers
in which heterosexuals in the heartland of America are constantly being infected by a single sexual encounter. The word
reaches us from our television sets as a corn-fed kid says from
a government-sponsored ad, "If I, the son of a Baptist minister
from basically a rural area, can get it, then anyone can."

Sometimes its hard to keep this world — the infinitely perilous world constructed by well-intentioned public health officials and business-savvy condom distributors — separate from the much less perilous world in which most of us actually live. A high school virgin tells me that she worries about whether she got AIDS from a blow job she gave at summer camp two years ago. An eighteen-year-old girl of average sexual experience at the University of Wisconsin tells a reporter from *Rolling Stone* that she's been tested five times and still worries. These worries are not uncharacteristic. They're also not entirely about the disease.

The extravagant caution — the virgins worrying about blow jobs, the factories producing dental dams and female condoms, the calls flooding the hot lines, the vast numbers of negative tests — reflect more than just the fear of a fatal disease. They reflect, also, the peculiarly American belief that a moment of pleasure is likely to lead to a lifetime of remorse. A friend of mine slept with an older girl in high school, in 1980, and developed afterward, alone in his room under his posters of David Bowie and the Talking Heads, the strange World War II era conviction that he had gotten syphilis from her. He asked his dignified, white-haired family doctor to administer the painful test, which to his astonishment came out negative. It's a strange story that has stayed in my mind, I think, because it so clearly foreshadowed our current ritual of guilt and purification: the negative test.

A graduate student in history told me his own story about going to the Princeton Health Services to get an AIDS test. "Have you ever had sexual contact with another man?" asked the doctor. My friend shook his head. "Have you ever used

IV drugs?" My friend shook his head again. "Do you have any reason at all to believe that you've been exposed to the AIDS virus?" My friend said, "No." Feeling called upon to explain his presence, he added, "Frankly, my girlfriend is twenty-two, and she's making me do this." The doctor nodded sympathetically. "Oh, yeah, I get two or three hundred of you a year. No risks. All negative. It's a new mating ritual."

This middle-age doctor is witnessing the larger desires and anxieties of these kids condensed into test tubes. Blood tests are invested with as much meaning as the silver pins and rings exchanged by another generation of Princeton students. They are, in their clinical, unromantic way, a statement of commitment. As the results themselves reveal, these tests are less about the realities of the disease than the fantasy — which is a peculiar and telling one for nineteen- and twenty-year-olds to be having at all — of erasing the past and starting over.

As we sit beneath a poster that says "Sleep Around and You Could Wind Up with More Than a Good Time," in the "health" classroom of Parsippany Hills High School in New Jersey, I ask a group of seniors what they would do if a vaccine for AIDS were suddenly announced on the evening news, if it would change the way they think about things. At first they look at me blankly. The smiles of relief I expect to see on their faces don't appear. Finally, a small, freckled girl says quietly, "Well, there are always other STDs."

The virus conjures up two different kinds of fear. There is the fear of the disease itself — the shortness of breath, the slow drip of the IV tube, a fear that we can barely hold in our minds. And then there is the fear that comes from the *idea* of AIDS. Although the disease seems to be responding to the new drugs that have been developed over the past few years, as cultural critics such as Andrew Sullivan have pointed out, and although it appears not to have spread at the rates originally predicted, our fear remains as vivid as it was ten years ago. It's a fear that rises above the particulars of the disease and floats into the cultural ether: "there are always other STDs." It's the kind of fear that clarifies and defines. It imposes order on the voluptuous chaos of experience. As the word "protection" is repeated over and over in classrooms, in magazines, and on television, it begins to take on an almost incantatory power, leaving the purely physical matters of latex and hygiene behind. It's not just the disease that we want to be protected against but ourselves.

The Girl from Park Avenue

The whole point of the story is that Alison Gertz could have been anyone. She was the perfect illustration of randomness: there was nothing in Alison's life — affluent, conventional — or character, also conventional, that would have marked her out for her fate.

Born in 1966, Alison Gertz grew up in the tree-lined quiet of Park Avenue. The patterns of her life — summers by the beach in the Hamptons, days at the Horace Mann School, one of the best private schools in the city, and nights careening downtown in taxis with her friends — were those of privileged New York. Her mother had founded a chain of clothing stores called Tennis Lady, which tells you something about the way they lived. The moral of the fable that grew up around Alison, as it was told in magazines and on *Oprah*, would hinge on the precise details of her class origins. Her tragedy was subtly cast as a cautionary tale about the dangers of straying outside the acceptable borders of a conventional middle-class — in Alison's case, upper-middle-class — world. Alison Gertz would become one of the late-eighties icons of how *not* to lead your life. And if you came from a certain place at a certain time, her story would take on legendary proportions. The social implications of what happened would be evoked over and over by the college students who were her contemporaries and the high school students who came afterward. But I am getting ahead of myself.

Pretty and popular, Alison might have been a cheerleader if she had come from a less urban milieu. As it was, she dressed up in low-cut black dresses, dark red lipstick, and lots of eye makeup and went, along with everyone else, to Studio 54 on weekend nights. In the early eighties, going to "Studio" was the thing to do for the city's fashionable young, and Alison, who became "Ali" as we slipped into greater intimacy with her, was not the kind of teenager who stayed home on Saturday nights to brood and write poetry. She came from that rare and envied species of graceful sixteen-year-olds who wear the right clothes and sit at the right table in the school cafeteria. Silver-framed snapshots of her girlfriends, smiling, their arms around each other, cluttered her bedroom, and she had her own small boat, the *Ali Cat*, out in the Hamptons. As we were frequently reminded, Alison also had a dog named Sake and a cat named Sambuca, which implied a precocious and ironical attitude toward alcohol and the lifestyle that went along with it. Although Alison would later describe herself as "not at all promiscuous," she was part of a world where sex came, along with other things, very easily to the very young.

The extent of Alison's wildness was, in truth, fairly limited. She lost her virginity at fifteen, but that was only when she considered herself "very much in love" and only after consulting her unusually open mother about birth control. She went out a lot. She tried cocaine. She left high school to try to be a model. Then she grew up and settled down. She stopped "doing the club scene," started having serious relationships, and went to the Parsons School of Design to study art. In the summer of 1988, after lingering fevers and stomach problems, and after an arduous series of tests, she was diagnosed, to everyone's tremendous disbelief, with the AIDS virus. She went over her list of boyfriends, a "short list" as she would later emphasize, and there was only one man it could have been, a bartender named Cort Brown from her Studio 54 days. They had spent only one night together. It was in 1982, before there was really a word for AIDS, when the strange new cancer was barely even a whisper outside the gay community. She was sixteen years old. It turned out that the bartender had died a few years before, and it also turned out that he had been bisexual.

The only thing we will ever know about Cort Brown, which sounds as if it might not have been his real name, was that he died alone. Even his mother wouldn't claim his body. There were, by this time, too many Cort Browns for there to be a "Cort Brown Story." Although he may have been as photogenic as Alison, his story, with its drifting and its bisexuality, didn't lend itself as easily to sympathetic print. We'll never know why he came to New York or what he did there. A particularly telling memorial called "The Faces of AIDS," which appeared in the editorial section of the *New York Times*, began, "Alison Gertz was one and that of the young man who infected her, dead years ago, is another." Apparently one of the "faces of AIDS" wasn't worth attaching a name to. So Cort Brown died "the young man who infected her," just a footnote to the story of Alison Gertz.

I remember when Alison Gertz's story hit the papers because my mother clipped out all the articles and sent them to me — a cautionary tale that would speak for itself. I remember barely reading them, crumpling them in the back of a desk drawer and dismissing my mother's mentions of them — "Did you see what happened to her? You should be careful." — with an impatient, *I know, I know.* There was nonetheless a sort of murmur among my friends about Alison Gertz. We were in college and almost entirely out of touch with the world beyond our gossip and classes, but other mothers had the same idea as my own, and the story had somehow gotten through. "Bartenders, no, not me," most of us said to our mothers and to each other. "I didn't really hang out in those kinds of clubs." But we had all taken our own risks before we had known that's what they were. It's true that I hadn't slept with bartenders from Studio 54 or Nell's or Area or Danceteria, or any of the other clubs that were fashionable when I was fifteen or sixteen, but at the time I would have considered that a failing. There but for the grace of God.

Meanwhile Alison was quickly becoming a self-made symbol of heterosexual transmission. The media feasted on her newsworthiness, seeing from the beginning the perfect headlines that could be spun from a story with such an unexpected twist. It wasn't just that she was twenty-two and beautiful and dying, but that she was dying of a disease that she was, in some vague and complicated way, responsible for. "Champagne, Roses . . . and AIDS" was the title of *Mademoiselle*'s long profile that focused on the pressing question of how Alison was handling "the double burden: AIDS . . . and fame." *Esquire* named her 1989's Woman of the Year. Legs pulled to her chest, head tilted, Alison looked out with her dark eyes, sad and quizzical, from the cover of *People,* which ran a story beginning in big bold letters: "Statistics said it couldn't happen." (Later there would be complaints about why Alison was arousing so much more sympathy than other, less startling victims of the disease, the most visible of which was an op-ed piece in the *New York Times* by a man whose brother was dying of AIDS bitterly calling Alison "an AIDS martyr the media can love.") The culmination of all the publicity Alison generated was an ABC movie called *Something to Live For: The Alison Gertz Story,* starring a pouting Molly Ringwald as Alison, which began dramatically with a deep echoing voice proclaiming, "If you or anyone you love is sexually active, this could be the most important movie you will ever see."

For her own part, Alison hurled herself into AIDS education. She became a walking, breathing illustration of the sheer proximity of the disease: one night lived differently, and there you'd be. Lecturing to high school and college students, Alison used her old aura of popularity — which teenagers can sense like animals — to tell them that "this is the time when the cool thing is not to have sex." Toward the end of her life, Alison became so infused with the "positive thinking" she got from books with the word "miracle" in their titles that she turned out to be a somewhat difficult symbol. She was so optimistic in her delivery of her story that after she spoke at Fieldston, a private school in New York, the school felt it necessary to write letters home to students and parents saying that although it was inspirational to see Alison so optimistic, they wanted the students to understand that her illness was actually quite serious. Alison would talk about her disease as a "gift" and about how wonderful it was that she had this "wonderful new career" educating people about AIDS to such an extent that she made even Oprah Winfrey raise her eyebrows. We do want our tragic heroines to display an appropriate sense of their own tragedy.

Alison's safe sex campaign slogan, "AIDS can happen to anyone," may have had a democratic ring to it, but the point was precisely that Alison wasn't just anyone. In her case "anyone" was a euphemism for "even the rich." Alison's slogan reflects her astonishment and ours: how could something like this happen to someone like her? "UNLIKELY SUFFERER" ran the headline in the *New York Times,* the implication being that here was a young woman unlikely to suffer from anything. The surprise of Alison's disease was that privilege, money, education, and good family all failed to protect her. In spite of the much-discussed, almost mystical security of the words "Park Avenue" and all that they conjure up, Alison managed to do something dangerous and to get caught at it.

In the movie Alison goes to a support group for women with AIDS at the urging of her family doctor. When she opens the door, which is significantly, almost implausibly, chipped, the women inside the smoke-filled room have heavy eye makeup and pouffy hairstyles; they speak in the frank, brassy tones of a different New York than the one Alison grew up in. She closes the door immediately. "I don't belong there!" she shrieks at her mother back in the car. "Those women in there — I have nothing in common with them. Nothing!" What is surprising is that the movie is uncritical of Alison's reaction. She never learns, as one might expect after an outburst of such flagrant snobbery, that she *does* have something in common with those women after all. The television audience was meant to be as outraged as Alison; we were supposed to feel, in the words of one of the first *New York Times* pieces, that "Alison L. Gertz wasn't supposed to get AIDS."

When a young woman like Alison — in the prime of life, with all the advantages — gets sick, it quickly becomes society's disease. It becomes an occasion for public soul-searching. For one thing, Alison's story follows the familiar plot of the Poor Little Rich Girl who has everything and nothing. Her parents' crucial absence is, however respectfully, made much of. In showing Alison's parents rushing off to a tennis match while she is trembling and sweating with fever, the movie conveys a gentle suggestion of neglect. And Oprah, never one for discretion, asked Alison outright if her parents should really have left a sixteen-year-old all alone while they traveled through Europe. "Oh," Alison said loyally, rising to their defense, "I was a very sophisticated sixteen-year-old." But we were left with the impression that her parents weren't taking care of her, that they were somehow responsible for what happened in their large, empty apartment with a man they would distinctly not have approved of. An angry letter to *People* put the accusation most straightforwardly: "AIDS did not take away the promise of Ali Gertz' life, her parents did that with their neglect and indifference." Her parents' permissiveness, which reflects the more general permissiveness of the culture toward its teenagers, had become, by a certain calculus, the true malaise.

In the movie Alison's mother blames herself for being a "modern liberal-minded working mother" and taking her fifteen-year-old daughter to the gynecologist to get birth control pills when she announced that she was ready to have sex. "She was a child," she says to her husband, tears streaming down her face in an agony of self-reproach. "She seemed sophisticated, but she was a child, and where was I? I was busy. I was working. I had no time to be a mother."

In understanding what went wrong, Alison's "sophistication" was frequently mentioned. It was Alison's precocity, and that of American teenagers in general, that seemed to be at the heart of the problem. Her disease, then, became the fault of the whole consumer world: cosmetics, Bloomingdale's, MTV, Studio 54, and everything else that conspired to make the young Alison Gertz seem sophisticated when she was really, in the words of the TV docudrama, just a child. It was also her mother's fault for working. Along with this torrent of social criticism came an undercurrent of nostalgia for a simpler age, when mothers were just mothers and children were just children; before children traipsed around discos until four in the morning in silky black stockings and high heels, and before mothers were too busy running businesses to worry about them.

Although it couldn't exactly be said, Alison was the "us" in a disease that was beginning to seem as if it was really only affecting "them." Despite the fact that Alison was living differently than most of the American public, with her Park Avenue address and her trips to Europe, she was still considered by the media to be part of the broader "us." She fulfilled the middle-class ideals that separate the pursuit of respectability, which is "us," from the perceived aberrations of poverty, drugs, and homosexuality, which is "them." Unlike the young gay men all over the country who had been dying of the disease for years, Alison's infection seemed to offer a vivid argument that the virus was finally spreading into the "general population." "People can't turn the page on me," Alison herself said, with an eerie understanding that her life was turning into a newspaper story.

With each retelling, Alison was becoming sweeter and blander. *People* showed her in her lace and rose chintz bedroom dreaming about "love, marriage, and a happy home filled with children and pets." Even the *New York Times* portrayed her as a sort of Miss America manqué: "Her goals had been simple, 'I wanted a house and kids and animals and to paint my paintings.'" In the two-dimensional world of the press, she was becoming almost aggressively girl-next-doorish. With its big fluffy pillows and cutely named pets, adoring friends and family, and simple goals, Alison's whole life was condensed into the essence of American girlhood. She was the living picture of innocence, except for one fact that was hard to get around: she had sex with a bartender from a nightclub at age 16.

So as to project a slightly modified version of all-American innocence, Alison had to keep saying, "It was not a one-night stand," though of course technically it was. The night when she was infected was by every account "romantic," and this is important to the story. The story, told in the breathy tones of teenage superlatives, begins, "He was the most beautiful man that she had ever seen." The events of the night are all soft-focus: the dancing, the kissing by the fire, the satin dress falling off her shoulders, could all be the lush imaginings of Judith Krantz. In order to create a socially acceptable version of a sixteen-year-old's life, the sex itself had to be airbrushed, stylized, glossed over, and avoided.

The most vivid aspect of Alison's character as it was revealed to us by the media was that she wanted love not sex, romance not thrills. Evoking the high romance and old-fashioned courtship of another era, the champagne and roses became recurring leitmotivs in Alison's story. Women's magazines couldn't resist the scenic drama they added, as if the more glamorous the evening, the sadder the outcome. And even the *New York Times* would feel called upon to put the champagne and roses prominently into their sober black-and-white news item. Part of the news, after all, was that the virus had entered traditional heterosexual relations. In the end the champagne and roses kept the story civilized. They kept it out of the flashing, drug-dusted world of Studio 54. Most important, the coy symbols blotted out one of the more unsettling aspects of the story: the sudden vision of sixteen-year-old girls all over the country fucking older men they barely knew. (Later Alison would amend her account of the "romantic" night: "He was so coked out, he just couldn't have an orgasm. . . . The sex was terrible.")

In America at the end of the twentieth century, a sixteen-year-old having sex is not particularly shocking. A sixteen-year-old having sex with a bartender from a nightclub is. But the media's discomfort with this element of Alison's experience remained largely unarticulated. As class isn't supposed to exist in this country of Jay Gatsbys and Horatio Algers, it's extremely difficult to discuss it when it comes up. For the young Alison Gertz, part of the bartender's thrill was that he *was* a bartender. He lived somewhere outside the large, airy, highly upholstered Park and Fifth Avenue apartments of her friends.

"He had this devil-may-care kind of attitude," she confessed to *Mademoiselle,* "and I couldn't take my eyes off of him." There was a nebulousness surrounding his life, unlike the boys she went to school with who complained about their English teachers, went with their families to the same sort of summer places, and drove the same sort of cars. What was stirring was the unknown. The cross-class taboo gave their prolonged flirtation an extra frisson — "All alone in that big Park Avenue apartment," teases the bartender in the movie with just a hint of class hatred — and that, combined with a more run-of-the-mill adolescent rebellion, was what led Alison to invite him back to her parents' apartment while they were away in Europe.

There are a few tender years when most of us, from the point of view of today's health educators, are too open for our own good. When I was young, sex seemed to many of us like traveling: you could see the insides of different apartments, eat breakfast in coffee shops in other neighborhoods, and generally see the way other people lived their lives — and then slip back into your own. It was an experiment, an escape, a way of playing at being something you were not. Part of the allure of the vanished world of Studio 54, the pulsating music and flashing colored lights, was the mixing and mingling, the democracy of drugs and looks. There was always the possibility of dancing with a stranger and maybe more, the possibility of leaving your own world — Park Avenue and high school, in Alison's case — for the rhythm and glamour of the moment.

"I was a little afraid of him," Alison told Oprah Winfrey and millions of Americans. "He was just so different from anyone I had ever met." Different. "You know, a bartender." Alison was too well brought up to say "from a different social class" on national television. "He thought I was just this sort of innocent little princess," Alison explained. "Upper East Side princess," Oprah helpfully interjected.

When Lady Constance Chatterley fell in love with a virile gamekeeper in D. H. Lawrence's novel, the book's characters and its readers knew precisely why they were shocked. An aristocratic woman in the arms of a working-class man was a scandal. When Lady Chatterley confides the details of her illicit affair with Oliver Mellors to her sister Hilda, her sister replies with straightforward, old-fashioned snobbery, "You'll be through with him in a little while. And then you'll be ashamed of having been connected to him. One *can't* mix up with the working people." Lady Chatterley's passionate and elaborately described caresses violated the strong but invisible laws of civilized British society. But in Alison's case the class lines were blurrier, harder to apprehend, harder to talk about. Hers is the story of a Horace Mann girl who didn't go out with Horace Mann boys. She may have been one of "us," but as the story was told and understood, she caught AIDS from one of "them." Lingering at the bar over her drink, she had wandered outside of her crowd. In spite of its expansive democratic implications, Alison's slogan, "AIDS can happen to anyone," had an ominous underside. The darker moral of her story was etched in our minds: *stick with your own kind.*

Something terrible had just happened, in New York's recent memory, to another child of the same culture. In the throes of passion in the bushes of Central Park, Jennifer Levin was strangled with her own bra by Robert Chambers. Like Alison

Gertz, Jennifer Levin was from a "good family," and like Cort Brown, Robert Chambers was an outsider, though of a slightly different sort. Although he cultivated the worn clothing and understated manner of the Upper East Side, he was the son of a nurse with social ambitions straight out of Dreiser or Thackeray. The case was widely referred to as "the preppie murder," but Chambers actually came to be regarded as a social pretender. Jennifer and Robert hung out together at a bar sinisterly named Dorrian's Red Hand, and Jennifer's friends would later admit to not knowing much about the background and character of Chambers, beyond his superficial charm. "I barely knew her," he would later comment from prison. "I'd been with her three times sexually." For those of us watching closely, the dark theme of Jennifer Levin's murder seemed to lie somewhere in the contrast between mystery and familiarity. We understood exactly how she must have felt tripping drunkenly along beside the tall figure — the thrill and danger of going into the dark fields of Central Park with someone you only *sort of* know.

By the early eighties lots of people all over the country who were not yet old enough to drink legally were leaving bars like Dorrian's Red Hand and clubs like Studio 54 with people they knew only superficially. Through a combination of circumstances, the question of how cautious you really had to be, of how well you really had to *know* someone, had come to obsess the whole culture, from *Oprah* to women's magazines to the *New York Times*. Everyone was suddenly paying close attention to the rules: What was acceptable? What was a risk? But the sorting-out process itself was often taking place so swiftly that we were barely even aware of it.

I remember meeting a stranger on a train many years ago, drinking cheap Scotch from the club car, talking, watching the brilliant autumn colors fly by, and being relieved to find out that he had gone to the same college that I had. I remember the spark of recognition — the pieces of his past appearing before me, the colors of his school sweatshirt, the brick facade of his freshman dorm reassuring me. I remember thinking, *He is safe.* After our train arrived at Penn Station, we went out for more drinks. In retrospect my relief appears unseemly, not to mention illusory: just because we went to the same college didn't mean I knew anything about him, and all my social calculations didn't prove anything about his health or sanity. But that kind of snobbery — so instinctive, so immediate, so irrational, so barely conscious — operates behind all our decisions about what constitutes acceptable behavior, or, as we call it in its present incarnation, "safe sex."

Alison's story brought to life the most implausible tenets of our educational propaganda. "AIDS is an equal opportunity destroyer," the slogan goes. "AIDS does not discriminate." These are fictions that the culture has been embracing as truths for nearly a decade. During the years after her infection, Alison's Park Avenue background was invoked over and over as evidence that we are all equally at risk. But watching tiny HIV babies in their incubators on the news, reading pie charts in the newspaper, and leafing through profiles in magazines, we begin to get a different picture. We read in the *New York Times* that three out of four new HIV infections in 1994 involved drug addicts. We read in *The New Republic* that in that same year Hispanic mothers were ten times more likely than white mothers to test positive for AIDS, and African-

American mothers were twenty-one times more likely. "Everyone knows," wrote Susan Sontag the same year that Alison's story hit the news, "that a disproportionate number of blacks are getting AIDS." Everyone may have known it, but most people felt that you weren't supposed to *say* it. In spite of the best intentions of the sloganeers, this disease is not destroying everyone equally. It's affecting those in inner cities and on the margins — those who are most susceptible to drug use, who live in poverty — in much greater numbers than the Alison Gertzes. This knowledge, which we all have and don't talk about, has begun to sanction a subtle kind of class prejudice.

"Have you ever had unprotected sex with a man or woman who you normally wouldn't have sex with?" asks the *Surgeon General's Report to the American Public on HIV Infection and AIDS* in a series of questions designed to help the average American assess his or her risk. In the middle of the formal, bureaucratic document, the question is conspicuously imprecise. What can the surgeon general possibly mean by "a man or woman who you normally wouldn't have sex with"? The question really being asked is whether you are having sex with anyone who is not *the kind of person* you would normally have sex with, and that's where the official phrase gets slippery. "Someone you normally wouldn't have sex with" is a code: it means someone unexpected; someone outside your routine, outside your group; someone who is not of your kind. The surgeon general is really asking the Alison Gertzes of the world, "Have you ever had sex with the bartender?"

Americans tend to fall into bed with people who are like them, according to the most recent in our long, boring series of sex surveys, *Sex in America*. The country is made up of what the authors call "sexual islands," each populated by people of similar class, education, and background. If there were a giant blue map of sexual liaisons, the islands would be isolated, separated from each other by vast, churning seas of cultural difference. People tend to stay on their own "island." "It is unlikely that a woman from the non-drug using middle class will have sex with an inner city drug user," the authors dryly observe. These "sexual islands" are ruled by the bland conformism of the 1950s, where a Harvard man dates a Wellesley girl and a guy who works in a garage dates a waitress at the drive-in, where an Alison Gertz goes to the movies with a boy from Fifth Avenue instead of dreaming about a Cort Brown. America may be a place of class mobility, but sex in America, according to the authors, isn't and shouldn't be.

Alison Gertz herself had a certain awareness of this principle. Face-to-face with Oprah, in front of the cameras, under the hot lights, going through all the details of her infection and symptoms, only one thing seemed to make her confidence falter: the fact that the man she got involved with was a bartender. She struggled to make her relationship with him fit into an acceptable story of flirtation and consummation, but her words sounded strained, her laugh nervous. The camera picked up her anxiety: she suddenly looked pale and small. This was *Oprah,* arguably the most exhibitionistic place on earth, where no detail is too intimate, no emotion too private to express. Even so, the circumstances of her night with Cort Brown, and the motivations behind it, were hard for Alison to justify on national television. The truth hovered uncomfortably beneath her words: she had sex with someone she "normally wouldn't have sex with."

Alison Gertz haunts us, not so much out of any phantom sense that her fate could have been ours, but because she is our Lady Chatterley. She was curious about what lay beyond the neat rows of pink and yellow tulips in the middle of Park Avenue in spring. She was seduced by what is not acceptable. He was so different, she said. I couldn't take my eyes off him, she said. Without even knowing the terrible consequences of that night, Alison was doing something her friends would have considered dangerous. She was turning what others might have left in the hazy realm of fantasy or flirtation into real life. If Alison hadn't gotten sick, her night with the bartender would have vanished into her own dimly recollected history of youthful encounters ("the sex was terrible"). But as it was, that night became her defining moment, one that would be returned to over and over ("it was so romantic"). Since Alison couldn't grow up, she was perpetually thrown back into this youthful embrace — reliving the power and frailty of adolescent adventure, defending and attacking it. Because of what happened to her, Alison captured forever, as if in a snapshot, a sexual daring that was already beginning to vanish from the scene.

In March of 1992 Alison Gertz died. She was twenty-six. When Alison announced her infection, her mother said, "It stands to reason that you're going to see more people like Ali," and countless experts were quoted as saying that there were a lot more like her "out there." There haven't actually turned out to be lots of other Alison Gertzes who got AIDS from a single heterosexual encounter, but that hasn't dampened our fear that there might be. Years after we read her obituaries, Alison's example still has a hold over us. The *People* magazine cover story is still passed around in safe sex education classes, young women still talk about the television movie, and Alison Gertz remains a powerful symbol of the worst possibility. In spite of the odds against it happening, her story replays itself in our minds: it takes only one night with the wrong man.

"Know your partner's sexual past," health educators and videos and pamphlets tell us, and what they really mean is know your partner's background. Better yet, know what school he went to, the kind of parents he comes from. Stay away from the Cort Browns who came to New York from God knows where to be an actor or a model, to live in a big loft and go to parties, and who are instead mixing vodka and tonics for the underaged. Of course you never really know anyone's sexual past, but what the health educators are telling us is to avoid the half-light of mystery usually associated with sexual attraction. On a purely practical level, asking someone what they have done in the past can hardly be effective protection. (Who would actually say in the heat of the moment, clothes off, lights out, "I have slept with a few men" or "Oh, yes, I did shoot heroin a few times" or "Actually, I'm pretty promiscuous"?) The point behind "know your partner's sexual past" is more philosophical: We are not supposed to be dark continents to each other anymore. The more familiar he is the better; the more illuminated his past, the more like a brother, the more like the boy next door. That feeling Alison had toward the bartender ("I was a little afraid of him") or Lady Chatterley had toward the gamekeeper (when she "was gazing up at him thinking: Stranger! Stranger!") has no place within the pieties of safe sex.

Someone I knew in college met a man on the street in Cambridge and brought him back to her dorm room. She told us about it the next morning as we sat around exchanging gossip, and in spite of the generally promiscuous atmosphere, we were all incredibly shocked. A tone of moral censure swept across the breakfast table. "You don't know who he is," everyone said to her. "You don't know where he's been." We might just as well have been girls in cashmere sweaters and pearls talking about her reputation in 1950. Now more than ever we are supposed to seek out partners who are "appropriate," like passengers on Noah's ark — two by two, like with like — and ignore the soft, insistent calls of the unknown.

The heroine of Mary McCarthy's 1942 short story "The Man in the Brooks Brothers Shirt" wakes up in a train cabin next to a man she met the night before and doesn't entirely remember, amidst the dull ache of her hangover, how she got there. Fifty years later, we find this scene as shocking as it was to her original readers, but for different reasons. What has always been forbidden — falling into the arms of a stranger on a train, a gamekeeper, a bartender — has come to seem deadly. Not such a loss, I hear my mother say. But even without romanticizing what happened between Mary McCarthy's heroine and the man in the Brooks Brothers shirt and the whole thrill of unexpected intimacy, I can't help thinking that something *has* been lost. There has been a collapsing of imaginative possibility, a carefulness infecting not only our actions but our thoughts. The person sitting next to you on the train is just the person sitting next to you on the train.

When I am talking to students at what the newspapers would refer to as another "elite private school" in Manhattan, it seems at first as if nothing has changed in the decade since Alison

Gertz was one of them. (To them, Alison Gertz is "that Molly Ringwald movie.") They sit on top of the old-fashioned school desks, not in them, swinging long legs against the battered, carved-in wood, as if they have somewhere to go. The large windows give us a long, dazzling view of the East River. These girls are absolutely eloquent on the themes of *King Lear* and whether baby barrettes are cool, but on the subject of boys some of them seem shy. They have that strange combination of certainty and uncertainty that comes with being seventeen.

". . . There's this one girl in our class who sleeps with her boyfriend without condoms . . ."

". . . I'm really worried about her . . ."

". . . We need to educate more people that they might die from sex . . ."

". . . Last summer, I almost hooked up with this friend of my brother's, but then I realized he was too sleazy . . ."

These seventeen-year-olds want to talk about love and danger and blow jobs and college — and the brink of adulthood that they are reeling toward. All of this is familiar, but something has changed in the ten years since Alison was one of them. They seem more serious, more thoughtful. They seem, in some ways, like little forty-five-year-olds. One perfectly poised girl, still recognizable to me as part of the inner circle of the "cool" clique, says, "It's just not worth risking your whole life for one hour of — " She pauses. "Hoopla."

At the same school ten years ago, magazine pictures of male models with high cheekbones, and hair falling glamorously into their faces, smoking cigarettes, drinking vodka, standing by the ocean in thick Irish wool sweaters, were taped to the walls of the classrooms, anonymous objects of straightforward longing and lust. Now they are gone. The sexual desires of this new batch of seventeen-year-olds are generally less flashy, less celebrated, less reveled in, and more orderly. "I just don't think sex is something you should just do with someone for the fun of it," a tall, athletic blonde explains to me earnestly. Keeping in mind that the best intentions can dissolve after a deep kiss or two beers, these girls still sound more responsible than my friends and I did at that age, more likely to stay away from fleeting encounters with the first boys who smile at them at a party during freshman week at college. *It's just not worth risking your whole life for one hour of hoopla.* They seem less likely to think of sex as an end in itself, to fetishize the physical act, to put too much faith in it. Their plans, and even their fantasies, involve a newly responsible and appropriate exchange of affections that would make the mother character in any Jane Austen novel proud. Their priorities are in order. They're not about to rush into anything. They're pursuing love over "hooking up," real knowledge of a person over glimpses, and they're not about to lose their heads over a stranger.

But something unappealing comes along with this new caution, and that is the distrust of anyone who lives outside their social map, which seems to extend to private schools in New York, boarding schools in Massachusetts, the Hamptons, certain colleges, and certain professions. They have been hearing the slogan "AIDS does not discriminate" for years, but they haven't exactly absorbed that piece of wisdom. Instead the lesson they seemed to have gleaned from their official and unofficial education on "safe sex" is that people like them are safe and other people aren't. "Let's face it," the athletic blonde says. "I'm just more likely to trust a guy in a button-down shirt and faded corduroys." It seems to me that there is an oppressive orderliness to this kind of universe, where private school girls go out with private school boys; where you look straight ahead, act responsibly, and think about marriage; where you say "thank you" politely for your vodka and tonic without looking into the bartender's eyes. What is missing in the honest, measured tones of this new batch of seventeen-year-olds is Alison's recklessness, Alison's openness, Alison's "Why not?"

"Frankly," one of these new Alisons says coolly, pushing her shiny dark hair out of her eyes, "I don't think a girl from Horace Mann would do that sort of thing anymore."

Playing Around

"Because of the HIV virus that I have obtained, I am going to have to retire from the Lakers," Magic Johnson said simply on Thursday, November 7, 1991. It was one of those moments that is frozen and lifted out of time, a moment so upsetting that it is replayed on the news so that we can experience the shock over and over, a moment which people later tend to remember in terms of exactly where they were ("I was buying bread at a 7-Eleven," a friend told me), as if their own lives were suddenly illuminated and clarified by the lightning bolt of history. Like Alison Gertz, Magic Johnson was an "unlikely" victim. But unlike Alison Gertz, the basketball player gave us a moral parable about promiscuity on a very large scale, about having sex with lots of people whose last names you don't know. It was a drama that confronted us with the final act of the sexual revolution: even the rich and famous can't be promiscuous anymore.

The result of Johnson's blood test would force the country into complicated paroxysms of introspection, the implications of which went far beyond the virus itself. Magic Johnson would become the country's most convincing argument for the necessity of sexual caution. From a carefree basketball player who slept with countless women, and sometimes more than one at once, he would be transformed into a hero of responsibility and moderation, and that transformation, strained and difficult and fundamentally illusory as it was, mirrored that of the entire country.

As the tall figure in the dark gray suit was instantly transmitted across the world by the television cameras set up in the pressroom of the Laker Forum, metaphors were already flowering in the minds of the gathered reporters. Magic Johnson's announcement would be a "shot heard 'round the world," a "bomb"; it would be compared in scope and magnitude to the assassinations of John F. Kennedy and Martin Luther King Jr. and to the explosion of the space shuttle *Challenger,* although there were no blasts, no shots, no bodies. The violence that was being done was to the more intangible fantasies of masculinity that Magic Johnson represented.

Part of the reason the nation was so "stunned," "shocked," and "devastated" was that we were confronted with a side of Johnson that we hadn't known before. Up until that afternoon, the world had seen only a phenomenally talented basketball player recently married to a woman from his hometown in Lansing, Michigan — the man, in short, implied by the smile. But the news conjured up scenes of random women in clinging dresses and high heels stumbling tipsily up to his hotel room, champagne ordered from room service — a side of his character that we were not entirely prepared to connect with a basketball player looked up to and idolized by children all over the country. It was the story of a "role model" and of the whole idea of "role models" thrown into turmoil, a story that would be retold again in the coming years with different characters, a story that would engage the moral ambiguities of the culture on the deepest level.

The real and largely unspoken drama of Magic Johnson's announcement was whether the country would stand by him. His wife, Cookie, whom Magic would later describe as "the shy one," was worried that after his revelation "they would hate us." This was not an entirely crazy fear considering the attitude of most of the country toward people with this disease and toward what it perceived as sexual deviance in general. It was because of the fundamental rationality of these fears and the suspense involved in how the public would react that Magic met with his press agent, Lon Rosen, Mike Ovitz, and other members of what he would refer to as his "kitchen cabinet" to discuss strategies for the disclosure, deciding finally to "be himself." As it turned out, Magic Johnson's overwhelming popularity allowed people to put aside their normal prejudices. Johnson was too beloved and high profile to pass quietly into the oblivion of lesser-known athletes who had contracted the disease (such as Esteban De Jesus, a lightweight boxing champion; Jerry Smith, tight end for the Washington Redskins; or Alan Wiggins, second baseman for the San Diego Padres and the Baltimore Orioles). By the time the cameramen had zipped up their cameras and the reporters had clicked off their tape recorders that cold Thursday afternoon in November, something that would have been unthinkable five years earlier had occurred: we had a national hero with AIDS.

The country was, in the words of newspaper reporters,

"struggling to comprehend what happened," though from a literal point of view what had happened was actually quite simple. What was hard to comprehend was not the news itself but the paradox inherent in it: a sports idol who contracted a fatal sexually transmitted disease in a country with an incredibly complicated position on whether or not you are *supposed* to have sex with someone you don't love or even know. The story of Magic Johnson's infection exposed the minor moral deceptions and contradictions that currently make up our public life and forced a collision between two conflicting moralities: the old-fashioned moral standards we still hold in our heads, the outdated plots of black-and-white fifties sitcoms like *Leave It to Beaver,* and the more permissive sexual attitudes of the seventies and eighties. On the morning of November 8, the day after the basketball player's announcement, the country found itself in the throes of the most painful kind of identity crisis: the question became not just who is Magic Johnson but who are we?

Though Magic Johnson had not actually died, though he had in fact made a point of saying to the journalists and cameramen gathered around him, "I'm going to be around bugging you guys for a long time," by the next day the country was deep in mourning. While the athlete himself went home to eat barbecued chicken and ribs with his wife and close friends, sportswriters were already writing glowingly about his "heart," "spirit," and "legacy." A public funeral was going on in the papers. The Lakers' coach, Mike Dunleavy, announced that the Lakers would go ahead and play the game they had scheduled with the Phoenix Suns because "Magic would have wanted it that way." And the most poignant and psychologically revealing comment that Johnson made that day, "Everything is still the same," was virtually ignored by a press corps intent on dramatizing how different everything was. That afternoon the cameras flashed, as Magic himself would tellingly recollect, "like little machine guns." A few days later the retired basketball player flew to Hawaii. The ball was, forever and irrevocably, out of his court.

The favored metaphor for what happened that November afternoon would prove to be that of innocence lost. "Childhood ended for Jamal Davis on Thursday. It stopped abruptly for Mack George and Shiraz Hayes, too," announced the front page of the *New York Times,* the larger point being that childhood had somehow ended for all of us. America was discovering, as if for the first time, the existence of a fatal sexually transmitted disease. In the language of television broadcasts, we were "waking up" to the "reality" of the disease. In fact, it was not the reality of the disease, which had already killed more than 130,000 Americans, that had such a profound effect on us, but rather its presence in the dreamy world of palm trees and starlets, where Magic Johnson was said to give poolside parties at his mansion with paparazzi flashing like fireflies in the Beverly Hills night. Paradoxically, nothing can become real in this country until it begins to affect those figures who are larger than life.

Because of his talent, drive, and the pleasure he so obviously took in the game, Magic Johnson was precisely the kind of untouchable star who touched us. His famously dazzling smile was not "photogenic" in the strictest sense but was instead so goofy and irrepressible, awkward and open, that it suggested kind of authenticity: he was just out there enjoying himself. If Michael Jordan, with his grim pursuit of excellence, appeared to embody the competitive mood of the eighties as he glided across the court, Magic Johnson was the pure, childish spirit of the game. In the weeks following his announcement, sports columnists warmly praised his generosity on the court, his unselfish style of play reflected in a record number of assists. Johnson was not just admired; he was loved. When a psychiatrist pointed out, in an article in the *New York Post* on how to deal with your children's grief, that "kids feel like they really know this guy," he was underestimating the extent to which most of America felt as if they really knew Magic Johnson. We really felt as if someone we were close to had gotten AIDS, the three-inch figures on our television screens being an intimate presence in our lives.

If the grief took on an edge of feverishness and obsession that seemed to run contrary to Magic Johnson's own determined optimism, it's because the emotions had gone beyond the physical condition of an individual basketball player. Those first few days after Magic Johnson's announcement, it was not just the man himself we were mourning but the more abstract image of success that all of male America yearned for. Magic Johnson was living out the fantasies of the accountants, lawyers, car salesmen, and taxi drivers sitting on their couches and watching him on television. "It's unreal what happened," his high school coach would say, swept up in the prematurely elegiac moment. "He was a dream come true." And that was part of what was so painful: something was happening to the dream itself.

"If it can happen to even me, Magic Johnson, then it can

happen to anyone," said Magic. In his most often quoted line, he referred to himself in the third person, as if he were already stepping onto the sidelines of his own life. From the point of view of the press and of the country at large, the moral of the news story was going to be, like that of Alison Gertz, *"It can happen to anyone,"* although the cameras and microphones and reporters were crammed into the pressroom at the Laker Forum because Magic Johnson wasn't just anyone. In fact, it was the enormous gulf between Magic Johnson and the man sitting on the couch that made the news so striking, not the impending sense that "it could happen to me." Very little that happened to Magic Johnson was likely to happen to the man on the couch. It was precisely the abnormality of his life — the magic itself, the silvery stuff of celebrity, the thousands of women leaving messages at his hotel rooms — which he would only much later describe in detail, that put Magic Johnson at especially high risk for the virus.

Up until the moment of his disclosure, certain questions about Magic Johnson's personal life remained largely unasked. He was known for his discretion. People who considered themselves his close friends — including Greg Kelser, who had known him since they played basketball together as boys — would eventually tell the *Washington Post* that they hadn't known about Magic's illegitimate son, Andre, for years, or about the huge number of women passing through his life. In his autobiography Magic would later go into the mechanics of his discretion: he wouldn't, for instance, take dates to "public events" out of consideration for his fiancée, Cookie Kelly. He kept up appearances. "The shocking thing," a fan would be quoted as saying, "is that it happened to Mr. Clean." Magic

Johnson had in fact never been "Mr. Clean," but there was something about him that seemed to glisten and shine — a sweetness and polish that could easily be misinterpreted. He had the almost naive, teenage quality of certain basketball players, which is mostly an illusion created by their physical type — long-limbed, lanky, and awkward. The childlike bliss that Magic projected on court also suggested the innocence of the orange soda and sneakers he sold rather than the wilder life he was later revealed to have led.

Nestle, Pepsi, Kentucky Fried Chicken, Converse, and the National Basketball Association itself considered the benign image of "Magic Johnson," flattened into photographs and advertisements, a valuable commodity. The NBA's commissioner, David Stern — who had been partly responsible for cleaning up the image of basketball in the eighties and selling the game to the heartland — went out of his way to play up the childlike side of Magic's personality. The commissioner observed in a television interview that "he has that twinkle in his eye," as if trying to connect the six-foot-nine basketball player with Santa Claus in the subconscious of the nation. The higher Johnson rose, the more money he made, the more glamorous agents he hired to help him with his image and speech and how to project more effectively his "childlike joy in the game," the closer he seemed to the guy down the street shooting hoops in an empty lot. (Toward the beginning of his career, Johnson had a little trouble in the press, being labeled a "prima donna" and a "crybaby.")

Even though Magic Johnson was living a relatively decadent Hollywood life, he was at the same time the ideal of wholesome America — healthy, strapping, and masculine — and as such he would be a powerful symbol. "I hope," said Louis Sullivan, then secretary of health and human services, "that Americans everywhere will understand better today that AIDS is not a remote disease that only strikes someone else." It was as if the strenuousness of the sport, the discipline and skill, connected Magic Johnson more integrally to "America" than if he had been one of the movie stars whom he socialized with and lived like.

Sports have long been associated in this country with a kind of innocence and clarity. In a drawing room in old New York in Edith Wharton's *The Age of Innocence,* Newland Archer contemplates the corruption of politics and business and thinks, "Decent people have to fall back on sport." And to this day in living rooms across the country, the almost mystical sight of a baseball diamond or football field propels many men back into their childhoods: you can watch a fifty-year-old man in front of the game practically melt into the five-year-old he once was. And inevitably, some of the irrational purity that we tend to ascribe to the past rubs off on the athletes themselves, which may be part of why people feel that it's important to "believe in" their sports heroes when they believe in so little else, and why the sentimental story of the decent all-American athlete continues to have such a hold over our imaginations in spite of the reams of tabloid evidence undermining it. Sports heroes manage to get tangled in their share of scandals, such as Mike Tyson going to jail for rape or Wade Boggs confessing that he is a "sex addict." But athletes have nonetheless managed to maintain an aura of romantic ambiguity longer than other public figures like politicians and movie stars, which allows them to be "role models" and "heroes" in a country with only the vaguest and most shifting sense of what the role of "hero" might actually entail.

That a figure who lived as publicly and opulently as Magic Johnson managed to maintain even a minimal amount of privacy in the land of tabloids and talk shows and gossip columns can be explained partly by the relative delicacy with which sportswriters still treat their subjects. As Vic Zeigel, longtime sportswriter for the *Daily News,* explains, "You just assume these guys are having a lot of sex. But you don't follow them into bars. You don't write about their bimbos. Unless they wind up drunk in a fountain with a topless waitress and it's all over the headlines, or unless they go out of their way to brag about it, you just don't write about it."

It's not that the American public really thinks that its sports heroes are as clean living as they seem in their uniforms and as the rigorousness of the sport, and the images of their faces on cereal boxes, in milk commercials, and on chocolate bars, seem to suggest. Since Jim Bouton's *Ball Four* scandalized the nation in 1970, we know that ballplayers sleep around. We know that Mickey Mantle was a drunk. But our illusions about athletes have a remarkable resiliency. We tend to want our sports heroes to live in the 1950s, where the national anthem is played and people have faith in God, family, and country. And we have a mysterious capacity to experience the moment of shock and disillusionment over and over again like instant replay: the hero staggers and falls.

In Magic Johnson's very particular case, the images of his personal life we were confronted with on the morning of November 8, as we drank our coffee and read the headlines, were jumbled and confusing. The news of his infection was nearly always accompanied by a wedding photograph of him and Earletha "Cookie" Kelly — bright-eyed, smiling, stepping out of the church — the scene further warmed and softened by the frequent presence of the word "hometown" in the caption. The eye was immediately drawn into the photograph, as if the terrible news could somehow be borne away in a glorious domestic fantasy of white tulle, champagne, and wedding nights. Seeing the couple frozen in a moment of pure and radiant happiness seemed to postpone the inevitable questions of how Johnson had contracted the virus. (Besides, the caption beneath the photo almost seemed to ask, how could anyone make sordid speculations about a couple named "Magic" and "Cookie"?)

The wedding photo obscured the fact that Magic had, as he would later phrase it in *Sports Illustrated*, "done [his] best to accommodate as many women as possible — mostly through unprotected sex," as did the frequent and somewhat misleading characterization of Cookie as his "longtime sweetheart" and, in papers ranging from the *Washington Post* to *New York Newsday* to *The Times* in London, as his "childhood sweetheart." As it happened, Magic and Cookie had known each other from Michigan State, though there had been a steady stream of other women in Magic's life. (If anyone was Magic's "childhood sweetheart," it was his son Andre's mother, whom he had known since high school but "didn't have much of a relationship" with.) "There was this idea," a high school friend of Magic's would recollect, "that Earvin could never settle down." Earvin did have trouble settling down, and Cookie seemed to hover nervously on the margins of his life for the fourteen tumultuous years they had known each other. But the word "sweetheart" lent a kind of sweet, 1950s inevitability to Cookie and Magic's marriage that it didn't quite have — after two broken engagements, an illegitimate son, and countless other women — in life.

The photo editors, reporters, *Time* and *Newsweek* columnists, and television broadcasters were painting a more familiar portrait of a hero (generally conceived, as one *Washington Post* reporter would write of Magic, as a "nice man who marries his childhood sweetheart"). But the reassuring vision of Magic as an upstanding family man straight out of the imagination of a Hallmark card writer raised certain logical contradictions, as any schoolchild could tell. "If his wife didn't have HIV, then how did he get it?" a student reportedly asked a teacher who told the *Washington Post* that she hadn't known what to say. The nation was struggling with two images of Earvin Johnson: the one in the wedding photo and the one emerging, slowly and darkly, from the circumstances surrounding his infection.

It seemed an odd choice of words when President George Bush commented from Rome, where he was attending a NATO summit, that Magic Johnson was "a gentleman" and when Vice President Dan Quayle eagerly echoed from Washington "a *true* gentleman." The nineteenth-century word was not necessarily the term that sprang most immediately to mind for the Los Angeles basketball player bounding across the court in his blue-and-gold uniform. Like the reporters who referred to Cookie Kelly as Magic's "sweetheart," the president was reaching for a solid, reassuring word from the past to get a grasp on a radically new situation. The word itself betrayed a certain amount of anxiety about the possibly ungentlemanly ways in which Johnson, still a "hero," may have conducted his life.

In the weeks that followed, it seemed important to talk about what a hero Magic Johnson was. President Bush and Senator Ted Kennedy called him a "hero," as did nearly every sports columnist and editorial writer in the country. After a while the repetition of the phrase began to take on a kind of desperate quality, as if we were trying to reassure ourselves: *he is still a hero even though he slept around.* The papers quoted countless children and high school students saying "Magic is still my hero" and "I still love Magic," the larger effect of which was to raise the very real possibility that they would not have loved another man who had contracted HIV through a random sexual encounter. The subliminal message was that these schoolchildren and sportswriters were magnanimously overcoming the feeling that Magic had in some sense betrayed them. The mantralike repetition of the word "hero" masked a kind of uncertainty and instability, a faltering of the general conception of what it would mean to call him one. The stronger and less ambiguous words, like "role model" and "idol," that had formerly been attached to Johnson's name, quietly drifted out of usage. And there was also a subtle shift in the *way* the word "hero" was being used. Johnson's own doctor modified it to a "modern-day hero," and Johnson very quickly became a hero "for speaking out" or "for helping others." (A few right-wing ideologues and cranky sportswriters vehemently dissented from the idea that Johnson was a "hero" at all. Wallace Matthews of the *New York Post* wrote sternly, "Magic Johnson 'hero' cheerfully admits . . . he engaged in recklessly promiscuous behavior, endangering his wife and unborn child," and Pat Buchanan said simply that Johnson was "on the road to hell.") The larger question, deeply embedded in the bright jumble of photographs, interviews, and articles, was, How is a hero *supposed* to behave? The answer to which, as Magic himself illustrated, was completely and bewilderingly in flux.

A few days after his announcement, a *New York Times* headline read, "JOHNSON'S FRANKNESS CONTINUES," but from the point of view of much of the nation, Johnson wasn't being nearly frank enough. At that first press conference, Johnson declined to comment on how he had contracted the AIDS virus, and the Lakers' doctor, Michael Mellman, stepped in with the not very illuminating "I don't think we know." Rumors began to circulate that Magic Johnson might be bisexual, rumors so prevalent and widespread that they condensed out of the misty realms of hearsay and gossip into printed copy. The NBA, in the midst of what could have turned out to be a publicity nightmare, wanted to make sure that Johnson's heterosexuality got onto the airwaves and printing presses that constituted the nation's consciousness. The Lakers' public relations director quickly put out a press release saying that Magic had contracted the virus through "heterosexual sex," and the team doctor issued an official statement emphatic in its repetition: "this is a *heterosexual* individual who contracted this virus through *heterosexual* transmission."

Magic himself addressed the speculation that there was, as he put it, "something funny going on." Three days after his announcement, he appeared on *The Arsenio Hall Show* — dressed in a white double-breasted suit, looking entirely natural and polished at the same time — and said to his old friend, who seemed almost birdlike perched next to his bulk, "I'm *far* from being a homosexual. You already know that." The studio audience burst into relieved whoops and cheers.

This was one situation that united the conservative heartland and the liberal elites: no one wanted Magic Johnson to be gay. The "story," as it was being created and engineered and managed by television producers, newspaper editors, the NBA, and Johnson himself, was going to have to involve casual sex with a woman. If Magic's story was going to be a moral fable projected across the entire country, if he was going to sell caution the way he had once sold Pepsi, if he was going to be a living argument for the randomness and democracy of the disease and the necessity of moderation, he was going to have to be straight. In an important sense, it didn't matter how Magic Johnson actually had contracted the virus; what mattered was how it was going to be perceived. And although there would always be whispers to the contrary, the official story put out by the NBA and emphatically reinforced by the respectable media, was going to be that Magic Johnson was entirely straight. As even Larry Kramer, the gay community's brashest and most outspoken AIDS activist, put it, "This is one case where if he's gay, I don't want to know."

Even after Magic dispelled the rumors that he was gay, there remained a general sense of dissatisfaction, a lingering sense that we weren't getting the "whole story." "It kind of hurts that he doesn't really let you know how he got it," an eleventh-grader told the *Washington Post*, expressing the strangely personal sense of outrage of many of Johnson's fans. It was as if Johnson's infection had suddenly made the logistics and motivations of his personal life public property. By the same logic that required Hester Prynne to tell the name of

her seducer to the gathered crowd in *The Scarlet Letter,* Magic
Johnson's illness seemed to entitle us to certain lurid details:
the country seemed to be waiting for the *Oprah*-like effusion of
names, places, dates, and positions. Despite years of experience
with the public and dexterously managing his career, Magic
entertained the surprisingly naive illusion that after that first
press conference, he could "leave through the back door" and
"shift the focus away from me personally." The focus wasn't going to shift from him personally for a long time, and his initial
effort to preserve his privacy, and that of his brand-new family,
would ultimately fail. In a gesture of almost absurd literalness,
reporters searched through his press agent's trash. They didn't
find anything.

The pressure for information, for candor, for the "real story,"
went beyond the demands of ordinary voyeurism. The frus-
tration that haunted the news story from its beginnings was
a result of the desire for a kind of resolution that no number of details, names, and places could possibly give it. The
impossible-to-answer question "How did Magic get the virus?" asked so urgently and persistently those first weeks after the announcement, covered up more pressing and abstract
questions about how something like this could happen at all. It
was as if Magic himself could somehow reconcile the contradictions inherent in the story, as if he could somehow explain
to us how the man whose smile sells us Mandarin Orange Slice
and who is the subject of countless schoolchildren's essays on
people they admire happened to get AIDS from the random
blur of Marleens, Susans, and Debbies in his life. The strangely
misplaced yearning for some kind of moral "leadership" from
the ex–basketball player culminated in the *New York Times's*

uncharacteristically giddy editorial "Magic Johnson for President."

In the most painful pages of his autobiography, *My Life*, Johnson would finally admit his "responsibility to deal with this subject." He would begin the muddled task of explaining to a fundamentally moralistic nation why he was living the way he was, and of trying to reconcile the Magic we thought we knew with the Magic he actually was. "Some people," he would write, "can't understand how I could love one woman and be with others."

The strangest feature of *My Life* is the extent to which it's really about two entirely separate and fundamentally irreconcilable lives. It tells the old-fashioned love story of how Magic met Cookie ("after the first week with Cookie I just knew I'd marry her"), interwoven with the *Penthouse* Forum–style stories about having sex in unexpected places (an elevator, an office desk, an airplane) or with more than one woman at once. You can feel Johnson straining, in what would probably be the essential magic trick of his life, to put his opposing selves into a coherent narrative: to give us Magic the athletic swinger and Magic the role model all at once. The juxtaposition of the two created a kind of schizophrenic effect that may in fact have permeated Magic Johnson's life itself, and in some larger sense the fantasy life of the entire country.

"In some hotels you could open your door at just about any time of day or night and find a beautiful woman standing in the hall hoping to be invited in." Such was the world in which Magic Johnson found himself as a twenty-year-old rookie with the Los Angeles Lakers. Strange women would send cookies, cakes, flowers, perfumed letters, naked photographs, and underwear by way of asserting their feminine charms. They would call up to his hotel room saying, "Hello, Magic? I'm downstairs in the lobby. How would you like me to come up and satisfy you?" After a game the hotel lobby would be swarming with female fans, whom the players called "freaks," pretending to want autographs. To preserve decorum and so that, as Magic put it, "the whole world wouldn't know," the players would scribble down meeting places and room numbers and times, and the groupies would meet them later.

What happened afterward was not exactly anonymous sex; it was sex where one person was anonymous and the other a household name. It was in these hotel rooms that the country's celebrity worship took its purest form. To the fans, the athletes embodied a kind of masculine perfection, with their electrifying combination of muscles, money, and how many times their faces had appeared on television. As Magic describes it, these women wanted to talk about salaries as a kind of foreplay. "I sometimes felt," Magic wrote good-naturedly, "that it was not me that they were excited by but my checkbook."

Magic explains that for his part he needed women to "relax." "I treated them well," he says, although he never allowed them to spend the night. He expresses a preference for women who talked, not just giggled, and carefully explains that they were not all "bimbos," though some of them were. Many of them were editors, teachers, secretaries, and, in his words, "college-educated professionals." College-educated professionals or not, these women seemed to offer a kind of perfumed feminine subservience and adoration that's generally associated with a somewhat earlier era. In spite of the frankness about sex for its own sake and the explicitness of women sending naked photographs and pornographic videotapes of themselves, the world Johnson describes felt to his readers in 1992 strangely outdated, the more garish, desirable, and threatening for that fact.

In the lobbies, bars, elevators, hallways, and rooms of these hotels, we saw the sexual ease and looseness of the seventies taken to their logical extreme. These were the gaudiest late-night fantasies of male adolescence come to life. This was sex as it exists in porn movies — fluid, easy, and impersonal. It was like looking at an exaggerated and magnified reflection of ourselves in a fun-house mirror: Athletes are bigger, stronger, and more virile than most men. They throw harder, run faster, and sleep with more women. They live life on a different scale. While a promiscuous man from a more normal walk of life may have slept with a hundred women, a promiscuous basketball player, if Wilt Chamberlain is to be believed, has slept with twenty thousand. And reading the pages of Magic's autobiography was like seeing a distorted version of what goes on at parties and in bars, frat houses, and college dorms all over the country, which is part of why Magic's warning, "If it can happen even to me, then it can happen to anyone," had such power and resonance. Although almost no one actually lives the way Magic did, in his extravagant extremes, his acting out of fantasies (which involved things like flying in women from different cities to have sex with him at the same time), there was some tiny flicker of his behavior, something in the careless attitude toward intimacy, something about the mechanics and sadness of it ("I always explained in advance that I preferred to sleep alone") that many of his readers saw reflecting glimmers of themselves.

Years later, as I was sitting on the subway reading Magic Johnson's autobiography, a skinny black kid practically drowning in his down jacket nudged the kid next to him, pointed to Magic's face smiling incandescently from the cover, and said, "Bet he got a lot of pussy." "Yeah," his friend said, raising his eyebrows, "and look what happened to him." This exchange seemed to reflect the ambivalence at the heart of the story: the confusion was not just about who Magic Johnson really was but about the larger and more disturbing question of who we wanted him to be. There was a conflict on the level of fantasy, on the level of what little boys on the subway dream about being, their wildest imaginings themselves colored by the sense that his was not a desirable way to live.

The reason the arcane relationship between the ballplayers and the groupies holds a particular fascination is that it brings to life a larger social contradiction: the entire country also admires and adheres to two conflicting moral styles at once — the flash and color of present-day sexual encounters and the black-and-white images of romantic love from a bygone era. The basketball players were operating according to two distinctly opposing moralities: one from the fifties, featuring wives and clean living and smiling on cereal boxes, and the other from the seventies and eighties, involving an acquisitiveness about sex, women, money, and power. The players seemed to move from their official lives — their wives, girlfriends, and families — to their casual encounters with the same speed and fluidity as they did on the court. The married players brought the roses the groupies sent them home to their wives, the heightened romantic symbolism being somehow out of place in both instances. The confused gesture, and the emotions that went along with it, seemed to capture perfectly the position in which the young basketball players found themselves, their strange duplicity succinctly expressed in an old NBA joke that Magic relates in his book. *Question: What's the hardest thing about going on the road? Answer: Trying not to smile when you kiss your wife good-bye.* The prospect of these tall, powerful men sleeping with not hundreds but thousands of women in lacy lingerie from Victoria's Secret, whose first names they forgot and whose last names they never knew, seems ridiculous, depressing, but also somehow, in its gross exaggeration, the fulfillment of some ideal of consumption, some American dream of what it means to succeed.

After Magic Johnson's revelation, what was instantly and immediately at stake was the dream of success itself. The excesses of the eighties — the cars, mansions, stock investments, and women — somehow got tangled up in our minds as they did in the *Washington Post* headlines about Johnson's life: "IT'S THE BIG PAYOFF AND IT'S PERILOUS" and "STARDOM LED TO INDULGENCES, DOWNFALL." The strangely puritanical point being that it was somehow Magic's "stardom" that did him in, rather than a virus. The *Daily Telegraph* in London referred to Johnson's "chronic hedonism," as if hedonism itself were the disease. And cultural commentators as distant as Kevin Johnson, the skinny point guard of the Phoenix Suns, and conservative spokesman Pat Buchanan would see in

Magic Johnson's infection with AIDS the need to "return to traditional values." Johnson was going to be incorporated into a grand moral parable that would absorb the entire country as profoundly as any game he ever played against the Celtics.

Johnson himself did not necessarily see a moral in his own story. One of the most striking features of his journey was his absolute refusal to apologize in any way. Throughout his long effort to educate teenagers, Johnson remained adamantly practical, his discussions of sex notably stripped of moral judgments. In an interview on *PrimeTime Live*, Johnson projected his usual comfort and ease when he said, "You know, I had six at one time." "Six women?" asked Chris Wallace incredulously. Magic glowed with satisfaction, "Six women." Wallace tried to get Magic to say this was "immoral," to renounce his past behavior, to give the public the mea culpa it had been waiting for, and to follow the script of repentance that is still written into our public life, but Magic said only, "That was my life. If you asked if I had fun, yes I had fun."

The search for the "moral" of the story would take on an obsessiveness that transcended Magic Johnson's own view of his life. It sometimes took on a particularly savage cast, as in Bob Grant's assertion on his radio talk show that only through getting really sick and dying would Magic "make a contribution to society." In more moderate channels it would frequently be said that Magic Johnson was going to be an "example," that he was going to teach America a "lesson." But exactly what he was going to teach us would prove to be a more difficult question. Even on the most literal level, as the basketball player traveled around talking to students and giving interviews, the precise content of his lesson was shifting and elusive. He began by talking about "safe sex" and later learned to use the more politically acceptable term "safer sex." He would joke about condoms on his first appearance on *Arsenio Hall* and later learn to emphasize "abstinence" and "virginity." His book on safe sex was thrown out of the curriculum at a New York high school, banned by Walgreen and Kmart for being too explicit and inclusive, and criticized in other circles for not being inclusive enough. The *New York Times* described, under the headline "MAGIC JOHNSON IS CONSIDERED TOO GRAPHIC," parental complaints that "the basketball player's written depictions of oral and anal sex were inappropriate," the word "depictions" itself making the dry warnings seem racier than they actually were. In the end there was something flimsy about the basketball player's rhetoric, something nearly everyone seemed to find unsatisfying. The truth is that Magic could still have had sex with six women at once and simply used condoms. But condoms were not the point. The real lesson the country seemed to crave was on the touchy and evanescent subject of sexual morality itself.

One of Johnson's problems as a symbol of sexual caution was that he lacked the necessary stiffness and humorlessness. His personality, light and joking, would filter into the discussion. He would be himself. As a *Washington Post* reporter would disapprovingly point out, Magic told schoolchildren to be less promiscuous, but he then told them that he and his wife were "still doing our thing," in a tone so suggestive that it elicited giggles and cheers, without mentioning the condoms that the couple presumably use. His eyes would brighten when he'd say, "You didn't mind being a daredevil every now and then," and he generally made the life he led, as Chris Wallace complained, "sound so good." But the real problem had nothing to do with Magic's virtues and skills as a messenger, which were in fact considerable, but with the message itself. The reason he couldn't transmit a neat lesson to schoolchildren all over the country was that there was no neat lesson to transmit. "I've got to tell you," Chris Wallace told him on *PrimeTime Live,* "you're sending me mixed messages." If there were certain discrepancies and incoherences in what Magic was telling high school students, they reflected the fragmented values of the entire culture. In spite of his best intentions, his eagerness to help people and do the right thing, Magic Johnson found himself in an impossible situation: the ex–point guard for the Lakers was supposed to solve the moral problems of the day. Perhaps feeling the weight of that responsibility, he would later be quoted as saying, "I never wanted to be a hero."

Magic was, nonetheless, doing his best to be a symbol of caution and responsibility. He traveled around and spoke, served on the president's AIDS commission, was given a presidential tie and cufflinks by the president himself, resigned from the president's AIDS commission, wrote a book on safe sex, made a video, started a foundation, coached, and opened a movie theater in a low-income black neighborhood in Los Angeles — always smiling, always successful on these new terms, but he never seemed to feel entirely comfortable in any of his new roles. If Magic Johnson appeared to have worked all his life to become a role model, he seemed to be coming up against the issue of how hard it was to be one during a period when the script was so ambiguous. As he told Larry King, "John Wayne always rode out the way he wanted to ride out. You know, he'd shoot the bad guy. That's John Wayne's way." The comment seemed to betray certain existential anxieties about being what his doctor had called a "modern-day hero." He was looking backward into the black-and-white movie reels of another era to the heroes of a surer, more obvious time.

After returning to basketball for the second time, in 1996, Johnson made this uncharacteristically sad and cryptic comment: "There have been people who wanted me to be something besides who I am, but that can't ever work with me. People see right through me. There were all these times when I felt like everybody else just wanted me to be one thing and I just wanted to play ball." In fact, no one was really "seeing through" Magic Johnson, but with all the pressure to be something besides who he was (the words of the *New York Times* editorial "Magic Johnson for President" immediately come to mind), Magic's deceptively simple statement, *"I just wanted to play ball,"* seemed to be covering a more extreme apprehension about what his life had turned into. The irony is that when he finally returned triumphantly to the court in 1996, he would not be "just playing ball." Instead he would appear on the covers of *Time* and *Newsweek* as an image of "Living with AIDS." Magic Johnson would never "just play ball" again.

Around the time that Magic returned to the court, the news broke that a heavyweight boxer named Tommy Morrison had tested positive for the AIDS virus. With reporters thrusting microphones toward Magic for comment, he looked down at them with his genial features set in an expression of visible discomfort, conspicuously *not* flashing his famous smile. The most salient piece of advice he could think of to give the young boxer was "to keep on being himself."

*   *   *

Tommy Morrison was not necessarily going to keep on be-ing himself. When the sandy-haired boxer, with his tiny hoop earring and his fairly unsuccessful version of a goatee, finally stood up to talk to the press in the ballroom of the South-west Hills Marriott in downtown Tulsa, Oklahoma, on Feb-ruary 15, 1996, he seemed, in fact, to be following a script that had already been written into the culture. He said the by now eerily familiar words, "If it can happen to me, it can happen to anyone." His expression was tragic and stunned as he talked, in his ungrammatical southwestern lilt, about his "promiscuous lifestyle." He was what would later be de-scribed by the *New York Post* as "contrite" and by the ef-fusive *New York Times* as "honest, brave, decent, intelligent, appealing and remorseful." He had just come back from his ranch, where he had been in seclusion "reflecting on my lifestyle."

Tommy Morrison seemed at first to have tremendous prom-ise as a symbol. As his trainer tactfully put it, "He is the first white athlete of any significance" who had contracted this disease, and as Tommy himself said, "There's a lot of white kids who didn't look at Magic and think too much of it." In addition to his whiteness, there was also no ambiguity about his sexual preference. This was a man whose answering machine message had the sound of a woman having an or-gasm and his own voice saying, "As you can see I am busy," a man who was, according to the admiring assessment of his trainer, "the greatest bimbo magnet of all time." Aside from the thuggishness of his heterosexuality, it might seem that Tommy Morrison's roughness and inarticulateness itself would connect him more completely with the middle of the country. As Kelley, the receptionist at the hotel where the journalists stayed during the press conference, said, "He was just such a great Oklahoma guy. I mean Oklahoma of all places!" And as George Vecsey wrote in the *New York Times*, "Morrison struck a deeper chord in me than Magic Johnson ever has. Magic still seems to be starring in a made for television docu-drama." Although Morrison had in fact starred in *Rocky V* with Sylvester Stallone, there is none of the slickness and shine of a movie star about him. With his scruffy facial hair and baby fat, he exudes a kind of unglamorous ordinariness. He looks like a slightly bigger version of the regular guy drinking beer in any bar in America. He looks like the burliest frat boy ever. "You have this great look about you," Larry King told him, getting right to the point. "There's a wholesome Americanness about it."

There was also an American dream aspect to his story that might have made for good copy. Tommy "the Duke" Morrison grew up in a trailer park, with a Native American mother who tattooed boxing gloves on his shoulder with her own hands when he was ten years old. His masculine hero status was further bolstered by his claim to be distantly related to John Wayne, although John Wayne's son told the *New York Daily News*, "We've never heard of the guy, but if he wins the heavyweight title we'll claim him." Morrison drank and brawled, stayed out until dawn, shouted things like "So many blondes, so little time" in crowded bars, and his life was generally, in the words of a Scottish sportswriter, "like the lyric of a country western song."

The day after he announced his infection, Morrison's trainer told the *Daily News,* "He's gonna be bigger than he ever was. He'll be known by everyone now." The trainer's barely concealed enthusiasm speaks to an ugly secret about American life: all kinds of fame are preferable to obscurity. (The most extreme illustration of this principle I can think of came from the resident of Nicole Brown Simpson's hometown who told the reporters who descended after her death, "She was so beautiful. I always knew she'd make it.") And for one fleeting moment it did appear as if Morrison were finally going to have his fifteen seconds of fame. During that brief interlude when Morrison seemed about to become the next Magic Johnson, Sylvester Stallone would feel moved to comment from Rome, where he was shooting a film, "Meeting and working with Tommy Morrison was one of my fondest memories."

In the days following his announcement, Tommy Morrison's life seemed to be rapidly shaping into an American fable of redemption. "Don't pray for me," Morrison told the bewildered public, which to be realistic was probably not deep in prayer, urging them instead to pray for the more "innocent victims of the disease." Unlike Magic Johnson, the boxer was eager to cast himself in the role of repentant sinner. He was overflowing with apologies and self-contempt. "Don't see me as a role model," he said, "see me as someone who blew it." The *New York Daily News* ran a story with the strange and somewhat twisted headline "SAVED FROM A FATE WORSE THAN HIV," which stated that the young boxer now had "a chance to put a troubled life in order." Morrison himself claimed that he had settled down with his girlfriend of two and a half years and that his wild days in Kansas City were behind him, and Wallace Matthews of the *New York Post* would find particular poignance in this claim: "His girlfriend Dawn Freeman says she believes that Morrison has been faithful to her. That would make Morrison's fate all the more tragic if true."

"There is a whole generation of kids out there like me," the twenty-seven-year-old ex-boxer mused, "who have totally disregarded our moral values." He was less graceful dressed up than in the ring, his movements somehow constrained by the narrow shoulders of the houndstooth jacket and by the more civilized attitudes that go along with being clothed. For the sportswriters who had been watching his turbulent up-and-down career, it was hard to connect this Tommy Morrison, with his sad brown eyes and soft choked-up voice, with the Tommy Morrison who battered people senseless in the ring and, in the words of his trainer, "had a little problem with discipline."

The darker facts about Morrison's life quickly filled the tabloids: his brother was in jail for rape; he himself was accused of assaulting the mother of one of his illegitimate children and with cutting a stripper with a beer bottle because she had refused his advances. He had once, in the words of a friend, "kinda power closed on a date," and his people had to pay off the woman involved so that she wouldn't file rape charges.

Tommy was, in the end, a little too authentic. He tended to say things like "I've associated this disease with the ghettos of New York" and "I thought I was being pretty selective. I could tell a classy chick from a trashy chick." He voiced the latent prejudices of the entire country in an uncomfortably di-

rect way. He couldn't be trusted to say the blandly acceptable
line, and as a result Tommy Morrison was not invited onto
Good Morning America or the *Today* show, nor did his pudgy
"all-American" face grace the cover of *Time* or *Newsweek*.
In fact Morrison was not rich and famous enough to make
the point that the disease could strike "anyone." He was also
too honest, too open, too willing to say whatever it was that
floated into his slightly unpredictable mind. (He had this to
say to *Dateline NBC*'s Maria Shriver about the tragedy of his
disease: "You know, the type of money that slipped through
my fingers, with this test coming up positive, is unbeliev-
able. A lot of money.") There was something unlikable about
Tommy Morrison — some of the violence and the trailer
park, the self-interest and the appetite — that showed in his
face.

At Tommy Morrison's press conference, the sportswriters
who had flown in from Los Angeles told the sportswriters
from other parts of the country that there were rumors that
Magic Johnson was still sleeping around. And five years after the legendary basketball player's announcement, the game
goes on: the players continue to do whatever they do in the
shadowland between rumors and reality, and the reporters dutifully continue to take down quotes at press conferences, in
this case Tommy Morrison's assertion that "this is the price
you pay for living the way I did." But in a certain sense the
story was written before it even happened. Someone in the
public eye announces that he is paying a price for his promiscuity, the tabloids scramble for sordid details, and reporters
and editors and television broadcasters search for a lesson,
which is always about being careful, not sleeping with

people you don't know, and returning to traditional values of family and home. The news was no longer news. The reporters left the Marriott in Tulsa and drove their rented cars back to the airport. It was the day after Valentine's Day.

"Caution Is In"

It's lunchtime in a restaurant in midtown Manhattan. On all
the tables you can see the pink-and-blue bottles of Evian water
and the dark green bottles of Pellegrino, which have replaced
the wine and martini glasses that would have cluttered the
tables twenty-five years ago. On most people's plates are elaborate concoctions of goat cheese, tomatoes, and arugula instead
of steak and french fries. There are no "No Smoking" signs
hanging on the walls because by now the fact that there is no
smoking is simply understood. You can see how our obsession
with safety has actually affected our physical surroundings,
how bars and restaurants and cafés in New York have changed
along with the decreasing tolerance for self-destructiveness of
any kind.

The emerging ethos of caution has also left its mark on the
law: state legislatures have been clogged with seat belt legisla-
tion, bicycle helmet laws, air bag regulations, and antismoking
ordinances. Since the early eighties gyms have been cropping
up all over the country to make the pursuit of fitness more
convenient and accessible, and supermarket aisles are crowded

with promises of "fat free" and "no cholesterol." It's as if "health" and "safety" have become the highest goals, the most elevated and sought-after forms of human experience. The reassuring glow of words like "healthy" is attached to a growing number of products as a way of enhancing their commercial appeal, and more and more car advertisements entice buyers with images of air bags and seat belts and children sleeping peacefully in the backseat, instead of blaring music, shine, and speed. Risk itself is losing its appeal.

Our new fetishization of safety is, in part, a reaction to the general instability of the sixties and seventies. Some of it comes out of a sober accounting of the human costs of that period — the Ph.D.'s who are weaving baskets in Vermont, the Manson murders, the teenagers who took drug trips and never came back. And added to the anxiety of turmoil at home was the violence of a war brought, for the first time on a large scale, into people's living rooms. The news of kids dying in Vietnam, waving picket signs on college campuses, and running away from home somehow shook people's faith in the natural progression of things, of children growing up, getting jobs, wearing suits, getting married, and living relatively uneventful lives.

It's as if all the wildness and confusion led to a sweeping desire for physical safety, for seat belts and air bags, for antismoking ordinances, whole-grain breads, lowfat milk, running magazines, health clubs, and anything else that might protect us from the intangible violence being done to the American family. The glamorous aura that risk and self-destructiveness took on during the sixties and seventies may also have been the luxury of the rich economic optimism of those years, relying as it did on the belief that if a kid drops a lot of acid, and wanders around barefoot through Haight-Ashbury, and studies Buddhist texts, and drops out of school for ten years, society as a whole can support him.

In his famous essay on the Me Decade, Tom Wolfe points out that the freedom and craziness associated with the sixties and seventies began with the thirty-year boom "that pumped money into every class level of the population on a scale without parallel in any country in history." If people tend to go into a frenzy of consumption during times of economic prosperity, they tend to cut down on all kinds of excesses during times of economic uncertainty, a fact actually confirmed by the National Association of Swingers, which reported to *Time* magazine a decline in its membership during periods of economic hardship. Part of what may be going on now is the feeling that we can't really afford risk.

By the late eighties, the most ordinary and banal activities were suddenly being characterized as "risks." When I went to speak on college campuses, I was astonished at how many students conceptualized the average date between two undergraduates as if it were the opening scene of a horror movie. Dinner and a movie, according to this point of view, was likely to lead to date rape or worse. And the faintest suggestion that eighteen-year-olds might *not* need a code of conduct on how they should treat each other written into university regulations in order to avoid raping each other would provoke many students to say, with a tone of moral authority, "But then we wouldn't feel *safe*." How could anyone argue against safety?

But what exactly is the risk? If you look at the educational pamphlets slipped under the doors of college students across the country, you can see the specific dangers blurring together like watercolors. The American College Health Association's pamphlet *Making Sex Safer* warns, "Sex under the influence of alcohol and drugs, like driving under the influence, is not safe. Drunk sex is rarely safer sex." It assures us that "using humor rather than alcohol to relieve anxiety" is much "safer." Reading this particular piece of advice, one gets the feeling that the word "safe" is being used in the most expansive sense. The pamphlet is urging students to protect themselves not just from disease but from the risks that are in some sense an integral part of life — like the risk of sex, of trusting someone else, of losing control, of drinking a glass of wine when you're out on a date.

The moral fervor surrounding the issue of "reputations" in the fifties or "temperance" at the beginning of the century has now been attached to the idea of safety. If you endanger yourself in any of the more ordinary ways available in liquor stores or 7-Elevens or Korean delis, you are engaging in a modern form of sin. By smoking or drinking too much at dinner or by sleeping with someone you just met and not bothering to use a condom, you are actually doing something that is considered, even in the living rooms of liberal society, *wrong*. Perfectly normal people will approach a stranger smoking at an outdoor café with an almost religious self-righteousness. "How can you *do* that?" they'll demand, in a tone that means not just "How can you do that to yourself?" but "How can you do that to *me?*" And sometimes this particular form of zealotry gets even more extreme.

The other morning I went into a neighborhood coffee

shop and asked for an iced coffee with milk. The long-haired eighteen-year-old behind the counter asked, "Whole or skim?" I said, "Whole," and he said, with a tone of utter disapproval, "You know that stuff is really bad for you. You really shouldn't drink it." I hurried out onto the street with my iced coffee feeling like I was taking some kind of obscene and shameful risk. "Milk fat is the hardest fat for the body to digest," he called after me, the point being that even the most trivial decisions — whole or skim, a glass of wine or Pellegrino — are imbued with a kind of moral force. If you smoke a cigarette or order a glass of wine at lunch, people will look at you as if you were somehow polluting not just the air or your body but the moral environment of the nation as well. And in this new atmosphere, people who take what we consider extraordinary risks, people who are wildly promiscuous or inject heroin or drink so much that they pass out become the equivalent of the nineteenth century's Hester Prynne. To find risk or self-destructiveness of any kind presented in a flattering light, one has to look to Europe, and even there its status is increasingly shaky.

In 1993 there was a controversy in France over a young filmmaker who died of AIDS and the movie he left behind. The movie is a romantic ode to the idea of risking everything for love and to the idea of risk in general. While French newspapers rhapsodized about the filmmaker's poetic heights of self-expression, American critics for the most part denounced his narcissism and lack of moral focus. The premises of the movie, and of the filmmaker's life itself, were almost impossible to translate across the Atlantic Ocean. The habit of conceiving of the world in these morally charged categories — "safe" and "risky" — is so embedded in our minds, so etched into our consciences, that it was hard to conceive of the film, the filmmaker, and the controversy they inspired in any other terms.

Seventy-two hours after his death, the French filmmaker Cyril Collard experienced what would, in poetry, be considered an apotheosis. He ascended into the glittering firmament of celebrity; he became a star. All of this occurred in a quite literal manner when the autobiographical film *Savage Nights*, in which Collard played a bisexual filmmaker dying of AIDS, won four César awards in a tearful ceremony as all of France looked on from their living rooms. In the elegiac days following Collard's death, *Paris-Match* declared him "the James Dean of the nineties," and President François Mitterrand wrote a letter of condolence to his parents, calling him "an example for French youth." It was not Collard's looks — his scruffy dark hair, golden brown skin, or sensual, almost liquid, style of moving across the screen — his scattered writings, or even his film itself that made him a star, but the example of the hedonistic life he lived and documented.

The jittery camera records him careening through Paris in a red convertible and groping anonymous boys in jean jackets under a bridge, the lights of the city shaking gently in the Seine. The film cuts quickly from his sweet, passionate affair with the seventeen-year-old Laura to his less sweet, more passionate affair with a sharp-featured, blue-eyed rugby player named Samy. In French the movie is called *Les Nuits Fauves*, and the promiscuous tableau it paints does have something in common with the bold, improbable colors of a fauvist painting.

As the bodies flicker across the screen, we see passing before our eyes a life that is no longer acceptable to live. Collard represents an ideal of recklessness and abandon that's in the process of being lost. It's the spark of instant memorial that gives the movie its power and added to the dark secrets of Collard's life that would later be revealed their terrible poignancy and fascination.

In the movie Collard is Jean, a wildly charismatic filmmaker. He is seeking, in his own words, "stiff cocks, degrading gestures, strong smells." But in spite of his rather convincing display of sheer physicality, it's not really sex that Jean is looking for, but salvation, oblivion, obliteration, and transcendence. It's a search familiar to us from the loud plaintive lyrics of rock songs and the soft melancholy of Keats's words to the nightingale: take me, save me, destroy me.

Cyril Collard was only one in a long line of doomed, needy romantic heroes fabricated for us out of the glossy materials of celluloid, albums, and print. But our feelings about him and his particular version of doom were different. The audience — American audiences especially — watched Collard's offbeat wanderings, in his sleeveless pink T-shirt and leather jacket, with a new wariness. The radical freedom he embodied was no longer as frankly appealing as it once was. The disease that we knew Collard had contracted rendered his attraction and that of his entire life — snorting lines of coke, falling onto his futon with various lovers (sometimes more than one at a time), and sleeping late the next morning — more complicated. In spite of the frequently made comparison, Collard's rebellion lacked the power and magnetism of James Dean's because we were no longer attracted to danger and excess in quite the same way. It was harder to identify with Collard, the way a whole generation identified with James Dean, with his ice blue eyes and red windbreaker, because to do so was too threatening. Cyril Collard presented himself as the embodiment of the pleasure principle, about which we had increasingly mixed feelings. The vicarious thrill we might once have taken in Collard's excesses was shadowed by a cool contemporary disapproval: the inescapable conviction that he had gone too far. It's not the figure of the romantic hero, wounded and volatile, who has changed; it's us.

Onscreen, however, Collard's attraction as Jean is still powerful. He slips past his lovers, tantalizing, close, and finally unpossessable; he is always moving on. Samy sulks. Laura shrieks. Ex-lovers wind up in mental hospitals. Jean is so profoundly seductive not because he loves and leaves, but because he loves so absolutely and leaves so quickly. Slim and soulful, he is promiscuity incarnate — with all the quick charisma and casual cruelty it entails. As Jean stands alone on his terrace, silhouetted against the dawn, watching the orange- and rose-colored light play across the city, you can feel Collard's presence — warm, electric, vulnerable — and what made everyone who saw him fall in love with him.

Everyone, that is, except American movie critics, who were, on the whole, as hostile as if they were the ones Collard had betrayed. In the raised voices of scorned lovers, the *Boston Globe*, *Los Angeles Times*, *Chicago Tribune*, and *San Diego Union-Tribune* called him in chorus "a full-time narcissist," "infuriatingly self-absorbed . . . narcissistic," "selfish, self-absorbed, and self-indulgent . . . a narcissist," and "an absolute twit of self-indulgence." Which is to say that on our side of the Atlantic, we were not seduced by his kind of jumpy, impersonal sexuality with its utter indifference to consequences. The outrage heaped on the young French filmmaker, who was by this time already dead, betrayed a certain amount of anxiety. Collard's objectless, plotless lust ran contrary to the Hollywood formulation that even the most sophisticated and cynical of us carry somewhere in our hearts: you fall in love, and the camera pulls back for a long shot. End of story. James Dean, in spite of his drunkenness and mild delinquency, was a good kid at heart. And even our filmic odes to promiscuity, like *American Gigolo,* conclude with the hardened hero giving up his rakish ways and finding true love. Jean infuriates us by finding true love — Laura and the consuming adoration she offers — exalting in it, and rejecting it. He goes through his happy ending and wants more: he wants lots of happy endings with lots of people. And so it was our highest conception of love — final, focused, and absolute — that Collard, in the end, betrayed. He may have been irresistible to the ecstatic French critics who rhapsodized about his art and grandeur and passion, the implication goes, but we were too mature to fall for his adolescent pose.

More damning than Collard's betrayal of love was his betrayal of something we seem to hold even more sacred: safe sex. All of his dirty, passionate perversity comes together in a single, sensational scene that lifts the movie out of modern cinematic convention and obsesses every one of its critics and admirers. The camera comes in close. We see Jean in bed with Laura for the first time. The camera gives us flashes of dark hair, an expanse of olive skin, and the sound of quickening breath. He is having sex with her without telling her he is HIV positive. But *we* know, and the knowledge drenches the familiar scene — the young couple having sex, which we've seen a million times — with a startling new fear. We watch the long, voluptuous moment of possible transmission, infection and desire mingling irredeemably in the motions of sex. As Jean moves on top of her, we feel almost sick with the vivid physical equation of intimacy and disease.

Jean, however, "felt nothing could happen because we love each other," as he later confides to a friend. And as he utters these words, one can practically feel the safe sex activists tearing their hair out in darkened theaters across the country. He is voicing all the pretty myths that are said to prevent people from buying and using condoms: *we love each other, so it doesn't matter*. But the movie becomes, in the reviewer's patois, even more "controversial." Jean finally tells Laura about his disease on her eighteenth birthday, and after briefly feeling betrayed, she forgives him. Later that night they fall into bed in a tumult of conflicting emotions; he decides to use a condom this time, and she reaches under the sheet to remove it. The camera zooms in to give us a really clear shot of her putting it into a pink ashtray as they continue to have sex. "I want you to come," she says hoarsely, and we see the outline of her naked, on top of him, against the venetian blinds: this is love.

The French, on the whole, seemed willing to accept this wildly romantic formulation. And in the poetry of French newspapers, Collard emerged as a prophet of true love: the first page of *Le Monde* read, "With Cyril Collard, AIDS is no longer a question of hygiene and morality, but of desire and love." Especially for young audiences, Collard offered a release from the doctrinaire, crassly practical refrains of safe sex. His instant cult status was a measure of the general exhaustion with the constant, unvarying exhortation *"Les préservatifs pour la vie"* (Condoms for life). Life, Collard seemed to suggest, had something else in mind.

One might imagine that when *Savage Nights* opened in theaters across America, this shocking scene of recklessness would find a similarly fascinated audience — one that was so well schooled in the pieties of safe sex, so tired of the prim, cheerful illustrations of the posters and pamphlets that, in their heart of hearts, they would find it exhilarating. One might have thought that along with our obsession with safety would have come a fascination with danger. With a safe sex ideology that was so insistent, so absolute and self-protective — *wear a condom all the time with everyone* — being drummed into our heads, Laura's romantic abandon would seem to have offered a kind of escape: expose yourself. Laura exists in a feverish, alluring world of her own making, purely and utterly romantic, a world entirely without drugstores that you can swing by to pick up a three-pack of condoms. She says, all wide-eyed adolescence, "I want to share everything with you, even your disease." It's precisely because Laura is going against every suspicious, self-protective grain of our new sexual ethic that we might have watched her sweeping, stupid romantic gesture with a kind of awe. But we couldn't seem to shut off the public service announcements playing in our minds — "protect yourself," "everyone is at risk," "you are sleeping with everyone your partner has ever slept with" — long enough to allow this scene, the fumbling human beauty of it, to formulate itself in our imaginations. We could barely even watch it.

The peculiar power of our distaste was reflected in the

fact that *Savage Nights* appeared almost unbearably graphic to movie reviewers from London to Colorado, even though it is no more explicit than most of the sleek bedroom scenes coming out of Hollywood. "Be warned — this film is pretty explicit," cautioned the *Daily Telegraph* of London. "Those who are squeamish should definitely steer clear," echoed the *Rocky Mountain News.* It was not, in the end, the explicitness of the sex that disturbed us, but the explicitness of the risk.

Cyril Collard achieved a nearly impossible feat: he managed to create a sex scene ("notorious," "needlessly provocative") that shocked the virtually unshockable moviegoing public. We can watch almost any amount of blood splashing across the screen and go on happily eating our popcorn with fake butter, but not the condom in the ashtray. The movie showed us the slight danger we felt in our bedrooms intensified; it gave us our own recklessness magnified a million times. We had been trained so well that seeing romantic abandon projected across the screen was curiously obscene. As Laura slips the condom into the pink ashtray, Collard breaks through our layers of nonchalance and boredom and gets to the raw area of a new taboo.

It was precisely the qualities that brought Collard such adulation in France — his romantic escapism, his glorified recklessness — that outraged British and American audiences. Under the threat of disease, lively movie critics were transformed into public health officials, writing about "role models," chastising the director with language lifted straight from safe sex brochures: "This film should be rated 'I' for irresponsible." "It's preachment of unsafe sex is flamboyantly defiant and the last thing an international emergency needs to have on screen." "This movie is about as much use to the safe sex movement as a malfunctioning condom."

Collard, for his part, was not trying to create a condom. As he said in his own defense, "My film is not an advertisement for the Ministry of Health. In it I show human behavior with its mixture of grandeur and cowardice." Collard's mistake was to treat sex in the time of AIDS the same as sex in any other time, subject to the same lies, illusions, and misunderstandings. The true controversy lay in his decision to make a movie with AIDS in it that isn't an "AIDS movie." *Savage Nights* violated everything that we had come to expect from a movie about this subject — the air of moral gravity, the extraordinary display of graceful behavior from the dying, the uplifting message of social responsibility against a wistful sound track. When it comes to this disease, we had been taught to think only in terms of responsibility, as if, with the threat of AIDS, the imagination had closed down. Sex was only safe or unsafe. The human impulse had suddenly become as clearly drawn as the cartoon condoms on public health posters.

We couldn't really watch *Savage Nights* because we were too busy looking for the message. And the message, if there was one, was not really one that we wanted to hear: true love is not concerned with self-protection. We watched Laura and Jean throwing vases, screaming, and having unprotected sex under a bridge as the whole city of Paris looks on, and instead of seeing a larger-than-life romance, we saw a threatening lack of control. It may be that the grandeur of Laura's sacrifice bothered us because of its implied critique of our own cautious and unromantic calculations. "He's slept with a million people," we say to each other all the time. "I would be careful with him." It showed us, with a kind of reproachful clarity, the selfishness and prudence written into our new sexual ethic: *take care of yourself.*

Collard's life and art were engaged in the traditional late-adolescent flirtation with death: the dark glamour of the rock star swallowing a few too many pills, the poet sticking her head in the oven. But there are always limits to the flirtation with death; it's usually confined to a flirtation with the *idea* of death, and *Savage Nights* is no exception. It turns out, in the most anarchic twist of the movie, that Laura has not been infected with the virus. It's this single lucky fact that frustrated American audiences, that defied our need for tragic consequences. Which is why *Savage Nights* struck us, in the words of the *San Francisco Examiner* and the *Sacramento Bee,* as "wildly amoral," "a stylized exercise in amoral posturing." Because of its steadfast refusal to show us recklessness punished, *Savage Nights* could never have been an American movie. We couldn't tolerate the chaotic implications presented by a character acting as recklessly and self-destructively as Laura and getting away with it.

As it happened, real life turned out to be the better director, at least from the rigidly moral point of view. The facts leaked out to the public one by one: Françoise Giroud's bestselling *Diary of a Parisian* mentioned, as a snippet of gossip, that the granddaughter of an unnamed writer had been infected with AIDS by Collard. Several weeks later the writer, Suzanne Prou, appeared on a television show about the virus, describing how her granddaughter, Erica, had died in her arms at the age of twenty-six. It was only a matter of time until the pieces were connected. As the scandal breathlessly unfolded in *Le Monde*, Erica Prou turned out to be the real seventeen-year-old on whom the character of Laura was based. And she was, unlike the fictional Laura and like the stick figures in public health brochures, infected with the AIDS virus during her "brief liaison" with Cyril Collard. She had sworn her family to secrecy.

Once the facts were revealed, given names and faces and dates, the debates about *"l'affaire Collard"* rose to a fever pitch. His heroism had to be rethought. Françoise Giroud announced, "We have to destroy this romantic image." Other members of the French intelligentsia began to speak out against Collard and what *Le Monde* had glowingly called his "hymn to life." They denounced him, in the high drama of French invective, as an "irresponsible criminal" who "loved life but sowed death."

On our side of the Atlantic, vague hints of "I told you so" circulated beneath statements like the *Washington Post*'s "In the rush to burnish Collard's reputation as a rising star who died young, no one thought to point out that he embraced a morally irresponsible approach to life (a point that did not go unnoticed when the film opened in America)." But no matter how closely and bitterly debated, Collard's personal morality was not really what was at issue. It was, instead, our general attitude toward those who break the rules, drive too fast, and have sex with too many people without taking the proper precautions — an attitude visibly, painfully, in flux. Do we bathe people who take risks in a kind of sympathetic admiration, or do we condemn them for "a morally irresponsible approach to life"?

Even younger Americans, for whom Collard's persona seemed to be deliberately designed, didn't give him the natural reverence given other creative hedonists in leather jackets. Instead they fastened on to the idea of his artificiality. To hip young movie critics in America and England, Collard resembled "an ad for Calvin Klein's Obsession," "*Vogue* layouts and far-out TV ads for Calvin Klein," and "commercials for upmarket cars and fancy perfumes." We were so aware of the commercial manipulation of his image, the slickness and familiarity of it, because we had already turned against Collard's kind of lawlessness. It felt as if we were being sold the bell-bottoms or satin slip dresses featured in last year's fashion magazines.

An article appearing in the *New York Times* years before the film came out reveals how far America was from embracing Collard's filmmaking philosophy and his way of life in general: "Although there is no documented case of the disease having been transmitted through kisses, medical experts have been unwilling to say that the disease can never be transmitted through the kinds of passionate, open-mouthed kisses that today's love scenes often require." The article discusses the merits of a "return to the 'dry kissing' of the days of the motion picture industry's production code. That code, which was a frightened response in the 1930s to attacks on such screen sex symbols as Mae West, also forbade sexually tinged language and required married couples to keep one foot on the floor in any bedroom scenes."

We knew as we watched the chaotic events of *Savage Nights*

unfold that Collard, with his dusky brown eyes and boyish grin, was dead. At the end of the movie, he spreads out his arms, Christ style. "I am in life," he says hopefully. But he wasn't. His ways of thinking and being were no longer a part of life, which is why he was so ardently condemned (an "irresponsible criminal") and so passionately cherished ("the pure spirit of love"). At the height of the hysteria ensuing from the revelation of Erica Prou's infection, Romane Bohringer, the actress who played Laura, sensibly said, "Cyril was neither a hero — it was those around him who turned him into a hero — nor a bastard. He was just a living person, of flesh and bones, that's all." As tempting a sentiment as this is, it's also not entirely true. In his last filmed moments, Collard was busy turning himself into an icon of a fading style: the drifting quest for impersonal sex. He was rapidly becoming the embodiment of *"l'amour fou,"* the crazy, thoughtless, consuming sexual love that we were no longer willing to indulge.

Living in a world of much more immediate risk than the rest of us, several gay men have written movingly and honestly about the perverse allure of unsafe sex. In an essay in *Harper's,* Walt Odets quotes a patient of his as saying, "I can't see trying to hang around for a long life sucking on rubbers." Others, like Michael Warner in the *Village Voice,* have written tortured first-person accounts of the unsafe sex they've had and the powerful temptation to take the chance, even if the person you are with in New York or San Francisco has a 50 percent chance of being HIV positive: "There is no sublimity without danger, without the scary ability to imagine ourselves and everything we hold dear, at least for a moment, as expendable." But in the heterosexual world, where the risk is much smaller and less easily defined, expressions of similar sentiments — the boredom with safe sex and the whole cautious ethic it entails, the desire for recklessness, for rebellion against the rules — are much harder to come by. A young female writer I know said to a reporter from *Newsweek,* "I would never sleep with a man who wanted to use a condom." *Newsweek* didn't print it. The story on "Generation X" appeared, peppy and predictable, on the newsstands without her adolescent declaration. It had been edited out.

It's no surprise, then, that our own romantic heroes, our "James Deans of the nineties," who wear leather jackets and die young, are not known for the epic proportions of their sexual adventures. Our current martyred rock stars tend to be, like Kurt Cobain, conspicuously asexual. And those who aren't asexual are as cautious and diplomatic as President Bill Clinton when it comes to the subject of AIDS. Our most flamboyant sexual rebels don't even *talk* about unsafe sex. In the sleek black-and-white pages of Madonna's shrink-wrapped book of X-rated deviance, *Sex,* she includes, along with the pictures of female skinheads holding a knife to her crotch and suggestive Catherine the Great shots of herself crouching over a dog, the slogan "Safe sex saves lives." The orthodoxies of safe sex are not ones that Madonna feels she should violate — evidence, perhaps, of her legendary marketing savvy. We don't actually want to see Madonna throw a condom in an ashtray the way that Laura does in *Savage Nights.* We don't want to see this single article of our fragile, new sexual morality transformed into a fashionably ironic photo in *Sex.* It's not that safe sex is more sacred than Catholicism, more deeply rooted than our anxieties about sexual preference or race, but that unsafe sex is our one remaining sexual taboo and as such it has a certain inviolate power.

The same year that *Savage Nights* won four Césars in France, America's own unimpeachably responsible AIDS movie, *Philadelphia,* swept the Oscars in Hollywood. Both ceremonies were tearful. Both ceremonies ended up providing their version of the complicated, new romantic hero, the one who is infected with the AIDS virus. Whereas Cyril Collard's character is artistic, wild, self-destructive, and irresponsible to the end, Tom Hanks's character, Andrew Beckett, is responsible, professional, virtually monogamous, family oriented, and gentle. *Philadelphia*'s nights are not savage but civilized, with white wine flowing, dinner simmering on the stove, and opera playing in a spacious loft. Andrew is in a domestic relationship — perfectly monogamous except for one night — that resembles nothing more than a stable bourgeois American marriage. "*Philadelphia* gets the job done better than *Savage Nights*," wrote one critic, and what he may have meant was that this was what we really wanted to see. Having rejected the grand romantic myth of Collard's *amour fou,* we had created a myth of our own: the responsible, practically riskless AIDS sufferer. He is not running around groping men under bridges. Instead he is a character lifted right out of the archetypes of the eighties, a lawyer trying to live well and get ahead. Risk is not his way of life; it's momentary, fatal, and curiously outside his character.

Andrew Beckett's almost subliminal flashback to the time

when he was infected, the one time when he betrayed the man he loves, passes so quickly that it's easy to miss: the wood paneling of the courtroom dissolves into a dark rainy night, and Andrew ducks into the flashing neon-lit Stallion Showcase Cinema and slides into a seat next to another man. Shadows fall across their faces, and the sound of heavy breathing coming from the porn film fills the air. "I'm Robert," we hear, and the scene suddenly vanishes back into the bright lights of the courtroom. The fateful encounter remains nothing more than a quick visual innuendo.

But when I left the movie theater, it was that scene that stayed in my head. It is one of those rare occasions when a complicated emotional situation escapes from a Hollywood studio. We suddenly see projected across the screen the driving restlessness that calls us out into the rain away from the sweet man who brings bags of groceries home in a paper bag. From the point of view of a Hollywood story line, this situation is almost impossible to explain, a loneliness without cause, an anarchic, anonymous craving for something besides what you already have: you have found true love, and it's not enough.

Unlike *Savage Nights,* which is almost entirely devoted to the exploration of this theme, in *Philadelphia* the whole irrational search has been crowded into a few seconds. If the scene had been any longer, it would have begun to seem to the audience, by some peculiarly American puritanical logic, that it was Andrew Beckett's fault that he got sick. If the scene had actually been developed into a touch, a kiss, the audience might have been swayed. They might have begun to lose sympathy for a character so carefully crafted to appeal, as much as

Hollywood believes a gay man can, to mainstream America. In the strict moral economy of Hollywood's world, which is not, after all, so different from our own, any more time spent in the porn theater would have meant that Andrew somehow got what he deserved.

The truth is that we were more comfortable with Andrew Beckett's death than with his life. The aversion that the filmmakers so cleverly anticipated was not just to his homosexuality but to the risk itself — the infidelity, the night spent wandering in the rain. It was the wildness, to the extent that this sweet and fairly unimaginative lawyer was ever wild, that we didn't want to see. His death, however, like any well-acted death, is moving. And the movie ends with a variation on "happily ever after." After Andrew dies, there is an oddly festive, life-affirming gathering of family and friends. Adorable children scuttle around. Home movies of Andrew at the beach as a child play, in grainy black and white, on the television. People eat and drink and hug each other in the glow of domesticity. And the risk itself, the harsh desire of the night in the porn theater, vanishes entirely into the warm, loving chatter of the community.

Both award-winning movies seem to reach for something that movie reviewers like to call "the transcendence of the human spirit." But in *Philadelphia* it was the continuing attachment to the stable home, and in *Savage Nights* it was the continuing desire to fuck around. The peculiar nature of Andrew Beckett's story — that he got AIDS from his one random pickup in the Stallion Showcase Cinema — provided its nervous creators with a subtle way of evading the psychology of risk. Otherwise conventional and upstanding, Andrew is infected with AIDS almost at random, as if he were hit by lightning. He is, in the end, just like the rest of us. He is not a romantic hero. And *Philadelphia* is the movie we wanted in 1993 and we still want today. We don't want anything like what the French called Collard's "poetry of risk." If we find poetry in anything, it's safety.

The Sexual Revolution Is
Devouring Its Young

When did caution become so important? When did the mood of the country turn against the sexual revolution? Many people seem to believe that the sexual revolution ended abruptly in the mid-eighties because of the astonishing appearance of a fatal sexually transmitted disease. As *Time* poetically put it, "The specter of the deadly and incurable disease called AIDS has cast a shadow over the American sexual landscape." Of course Americans *were* terrified of AIDS, but the disillusionment with the sexual revolution, and the values and attitudes associated with it, was well under way before the fatal virus had even been given a name. If you sort through the shifting ephemera of the culture — the newspaper cover stories that were thrown away, the movies people watched, the photographs in their albums, and the old bestsellers that fill the shelves of second-hand bookstores — you can actually see the gradual buildup of anxiety over the past twenty-five years.

It's often said that the sexual revolution is a fiction created by magazines and newspapers hungry for headlines, captions, and trends. This is true, of course, but it's a fiction that nonetheless captures and puts into words the ineffable social changes, the millions of minute shifts in expectations and customs, that made themselves felt in people's lives. If you look at the way the mood of the times has been processed through magazines, newspapers, and television broadcasts, you can see the creation of a moral parable in which the news of the AIDS virus would simply be the final chapter. The creation of this parable began sometime in the late sixties. It was about how the price of the sexual revolution was going to be paid.

On February 16, 1987, the country entered "a new era of caution and restraint," according to the copies of *Time* that people leafed through at supermarket checkout counters across the nation. "The sexual revolution of the past quarter century" had drawn to a close. The magazine's readers may have felt a distinct sense of déjà vu, as if they had read those words somewhere before, and in fact they had. In 1982 *Time* had declared, "Herpes, an incurable virus, threatens to undo the sexual revolution."

Since herpes proved to be only one of the many "final blows" dealt to the sexual revolution, one began to get the sense that the different viruses were simply shifting particulars in a larger cultural script. "The days of carefree and casual sex are over," *Newsweek* declared, and it was the end of casual sex, rather than the details of the diseases themselves, that seemed to be the point of all of these articles. In 1987, at the height of the country's anxiety about AIDS, *Time* reported that "instead of a transfixed gaze, lovers may feel that they have to give each other a detailed grilling on present health and past liaisons." Five years earlier, *Time* had announced a similar change in "the romantic gaze" for a different reason: "With visions of herpes sores clouding each new encounter, would-be lovers who used to gaze romantically into each other's eyes now look for the tell-tale blink or averted glance of the would-be herpetic."

One couldn't help speculating that all the caution and restraint *Time*'s and *Newsweek*'s reporters had captured in their microcassette recorders had less to do with the emergence of a fatal sexually transmitted disease than it seemed. The murmurs of apprehension they recorded, the talk of staying home more and renting videos, of really *knowing* the people you slept with and trying to have stable, monogamous relationships, was a product of a sea change in the country's values. All of this prudence and stability was not entirely motivated by either herpes or AIDS. Caution had become an end in itself.

The early reports on the outbreak of herpes can be boiled down to two words: *of course.* The articles detailing the herpes scare were blueprints for the warnings of sexual danger that would inundate magazines and newspapers for the next decade. "There is little doubt," *Esquire* declared in 1982, "that the spread of herpes is part of the dark underside of the sexual revolution." If the venereal disease was intimately connected to the sexual attitudes of the past several decades, it was not just in the literal sense that more people were passing it around; it was that the sins of the past were coming back to haunt us. Journalists and television broadcasters referred to herpes as "the virus of love," suggesting that what was sweeping through the innocent ranks of society was not just an infection but an uncontrollable and feverish form of love. The euphemistic phrase "the virus of love" actually drew attention to the glaring fact it was meant to cover up: it wasn't really *love* we were worried about; it was sex.

One-night stands were the real epidemic. The horror stories about herpes in newspapers and magazines ("You wake up from the sweetest night imaginable . . .") were given headlines like "THE NEW SCARLET LETTER" as if the venereal disease made a sort of moral sense. "A Washington lawyer, 28, spent a month in bed with her first bout, then stayed drunk for half a year. . . . She stopped wearing makeup, ironing her clothes and shaving her legs," reported *Time,* and stories of other mortified swingers, penitent adulterers, and reformed roués were stitched together into a giant cultural parable of self-contempt. *Time's* reporters even managed to link the guilt the herpes sufferers were feeling to the declining fashions of the sexual revolution: "Since friction can trigger a recurrence, tight jeans, the uniform of the sexual revolution, are out." *Esquire, Time, Newsweek,* and presumably some portion of the American public were greeting the rise of herpes cases with a sense that their worst expectations had been fulfilled.

The emergence of herpes, an incurable disease that might stop a new generation from going to singles bars and falling into bed with as many people as they could, was, even more darkly, met in many quarters with a certain amount of relief. "Wives now give their husbands smiling lectures on the ravages of disease to keep them faithful," announced *Time's* writers. One can't help but notice that *Time's* own account of the "ravages of disease" hums with a sense of nervous satisfaction and ends on what seems like an optimistic note: "Perhaps not so unhappily, it may be a prime mover in helping to bring to a close an era of mindless promiscuity. The monogamous now have one more reason to remain so. For all of the distress it has brought, the troublesome little bug may inadvertently be ushering in a period in which sex is linked more firmly to monogamy and trust." *Thank God*, the authors seemed to be saying, *now things can finally go back to normal.*

Years later it would almost seem as if the media's script for the AIDS virus were written before the first cases of the mysterious new disease began to appear in New York and San Francisco. *Life* magazine echoed *Time's* point about bringing an era of mindless promiscuity to a close: "The fear of AIDS, by applying the brakes to lust, gives relationships room to evolve and become richer." The plot had, in an important sense, already been decided: the sexual revolution had to come to an end.

My own childhood understanding of the sexual revolution was diffuse and secondhand. It was carried in the music that came from behind the closed doors of my sisters' rooms and the sweet-smelling smoke that floated into the hallway. I pieced it together from the pictures in the copy of *The Joy of Sex* I found on my parents' bookshelf, the album covers strewn on the floor (particularly one Rolling Stones album with a real zipper on the fly of a man's jeans), and the sight of unwashed boys slipping up the carpeted stairs into my sisters' bedrooms. "It's perfectly *natural*," I remember my mother saying about whatever it was that was going on, her own skirts fashionably short and her eyes rimmed with kohl. "It's not really about *love*," my sisters would say. "You'll understand when you're older." But by the time I was old enough to understand, the revolution was already over.

The carefree way in which women of my sisters' generation went on the birth control pill and slept with whomever they felt attracted to is now relegated to faded articles in national magazines with photographs of suntanned kids beaming blissfully at the camera. But it's an image that still has a certain power over those of us who came afterward. The ethos of the sexual revolution was not, as some would later argue, confined to nudists, drifters, hippies, flower children, and college students. As early as 1967 the ideals of sexual freedom were so banal that the first sentence of a *Newsweek* cover story declared flatly, "The old taboos are dead and dying." The buoyancy of the new ideas kept books like George and Nena O'Neill's *Open Marriage: A New Lifestyle for Couples,* John Updike's *Couples,* and Alex Comfort's *The Joy of Sex* on the bestseller list for years. Even the law itself changed to accommodate shifting attitudes toward marriage and commitment, enabling couples to file for convenient new "no-fault" divorces, which made the whole process of shedding your old life and starting a new one as smooth and painless as possible.

One of the harder things to understand about the sexual revolution for those of us who missed it was the hopefulness attached to the changes in the culture. There was an atmosphere of optimism, of progress, of "open air," as the happily married authors of *Open Marriage* put it. "The sexual repression of the Victorian era has been lifted," the husband-and-wife team wrote breathlessly. "We must move out from its shadows into the open air of a new time in which men and women must work together for mutual fulfillment through individual growth." The popularity of their work revealed that the average book buyer in Des Moines, Iowa, seemed to feel that "fulfillment" was within his grasp, too. Pop psychology was offering all of America a utopian vocabulary through which to filter their changing experience. It seemed to involve the end of "repression," the lifting of "inhibitions," and, as *Open Marriage* urged, "an emphasis on the now." Even bastions of established opinion, like *Newsweek*, cheerfully called out to middle America, "The emergence from prudery and hypocrisy. . . opens up new possibilities."

In *Thy Neighbor's Wife*, Gay Talese compiled what was essentially a massive *Let's Go* travel guide to the changing sexual landscape of the nation: "As Sally herself entered the sixties, she was embattled but stylishly slim, wearing tight-fitting blue jeans, and rose-tinted granny glasses, through which she viewed the world with a rejuvenated sense that her personal liberation was within reach." If the newspapers, magazines, photographs, and books are to be believed, there were vast numbers of people who were standing, stylishly slim, in tight-fitting jeans, just on the euphoric brink of personal liberation. When visiting the Sandstone Retreat nestled in the luxuriant green hills of southern California, which was "undoubtedly the most liberated fifteen acres of land in America's not-always-democratic Republic," Talese wrote that he himself "was mesmerized by the place, its tranquillity and freedom, its minimum of rules and regulations." The retreat struck him as "a permissive paradise." (Tom Wolfe had a different response to Sandstone: "They copulate in the living room, on the lawn, out by the pool, on the tennis courts, with the same open, free, liberated spirit as dogs in the park or baboons in a tree.") But the response of Gay Talese, smiling and twinkling at us from the back jacket of his book, to the various manifestations of sexual freedom he encountered seemed, for a while, to be the response of much of the country. Talese was like a rabbit caught in the headlights of oncoming traffic: blinded by the light, frozen for a moment, transfixed.

The new era had in fact impressed many of its chroniclers and observers as paradise. To read accounts of the period, it seemed as if the whole culture was glowing with health and mutual fulfillment and the free and open expression of its appetites. We were reaching a "higher level" of understanding or moving onto a "new plane" of existence — a therapeutic vision of how bikinis from France, and the Pill, and nudity in movies, and honest and open marriages, and no-fault divorces would crystallize into the perfect society. But implicit in the idea of paradise is, of course, the premonition of a fall.

This new state of affairs seemed, from the start, almost too good to be true. The word "paradise" itself conveyed the shimmering aspect of illusion, the precarious sense that what was happening in this country in the late sixties and early seventies was not entirely *real*. The mythology of the period was dominated by images of people leaving their regular lives as housewives, accountants, businessmen, and students for more extraordinary and "meaningful" fates as swingers, activists, and mystics. Implicit in all of this was a promise of transformation: the kid from Iowa could suddenly find himself at the center of it all, in the streets of San Francisco, doing acid, with whatever happened to him bearing only a glancing resemblance to what we usually think of as "real life" and no resemblance at all to what happened to his parents. Life, as Joan Didion put it, had taken on the logic of dreamwork. It had an almost hallucinogenic quality that had less to do with the vast quantities of drugs that were actually consumed during those years than with the general mood of escapism and irresponsibility.

Right beneath the surface of the easygoing rhetoric of the sexual revolution was a lingering insecurity that penetrated even the "joy" of *The Joy of Sex*. "There is nothing to be afraid of," Alex Comfort wrote soothingly, "and there never was." That he needed to include this reassurance in the book that would be tucked in between *The Great Gatsby* and *Moby Dick* on the bookshelves of respectable middle-class living rooms across the country implied a certain amount of resistance to his ideas. Alex Comfort seemed to be anticipating the fear that all this stripping of inhibitions, and expressing of emotions, and leaving of husbands and wives and the whole traditional concept of families, was going to endanger us in some hitherto unimaginable way. The ripples of unease, barely detectable in the joyful sketches of liberated, naked people in *The Joy of Sex*, would, as the seventies wore on, take bolder and more striking forms.

Even in the opening pages of its own mythology, the sexual revolution involved a great deal of anxiety and nervousness. Take an instant classic of sexual liberation like Erica Jong's *Fear of Flying*. Although the young blond author was acclaimed as "the high priestess of sexual abandon" and "the latter day wife of Bath" and the book itself was called "the most uninhibited, delicious, erotic novel a woman ever wrote," it was in fact more about fear than about flying. Its sensual heroine, Isadora Wing, with her creamy thighs and her active fantasy life, is tormented by conventional visions of window boxes and picket fences. "I am really a puritan at heart," confesses the dirty-minded Isadora. And penetrating deep into the paradox of American sexual freedom, her psychiatrist replies in his heavy German accent, "You *are* a puritan, and of the worst sort. You do what you like but you feel so guilty that you don't enjoy it. What, actually, is the point?" The true strength of Jong's book is not the Norman Mailer–like descriptions of fucking for which it became famous, but that it actually manages to get the double nature of the promiscuous puritan down on paper: the uneasy mix of sin and virtue, guilt and fantasy, indulgence and regret. *Fear of Flying* is actually about the impossibility of sexual abandon: sex is easy; abandon is not.

The obsession with traditional morality that Jong articulates so clearly was part of the sexual revolution all along. This "new society" was so aware of its permissiveness, so concerned with the traditions that were being left behind, that the "dead and dying" taboos were still exerting a huge influence. The notorious pleasure palaces *Playboy*'s Hugh Hefner built in Chicago and Los Angeles, for instance, were only impressive monuments to the new morality to the extent that we were still under the sway of the old one. The concept of "sin," of departing from the conventional world and doing things others considered morally wrong and fairly shocking, was an integral part of the whole ethos. You have only to open a copy of *Playboy* from the sixties to catch, amidst the round breasts and lowered eyelids, the spirit of self-conscious naughtiness that runs through so much of what we think of as "sexual liberation." The magazine's frisson depends on the effect of peeking, of furtiveness; the words and photographs are infused with the knowledge that at any moment the magazine might have to be slammed shut and shoved into a drawer.

In 1967 on the cover of *Newsweek* the words "Anything Goes: The Permissive Society" were printed next to a naked blond actress. This snapshot captures a certain quality of self-consciousness that was a crucial part of what was somewhat misleadingly being called "freedom." The actress is seen from the back, her head turned toward us, mouth opened suggestively, as if she, like everyone else in the "permissive society," caught in a bacchanalian moment, is turning back to look at the camera.

Sexual guilt has been an integral part of the American version of sexual freedom since the nineteenth century. The phrase "free love," coined in the middle of the nineteenth century by John Humphrey Noyes, the founder and leader of an experimental community at Oneida, New York, contains within it a hint of escape, the knowledge that love is almost never free. Under Noyes's supervision, the members of the Oneida community lived in a state of what other clergymen called a "utopia of obscenity" and they themselves called "complex marriage," in which everyone over the age of twelve was essentially married to everyone else. But the bold experiment in abolishing sin was destined to fail. In a large mansion set in the idyllic strawberry fields of upstate New York, the members of the new community simply invented new sins to feel guilty for: the "claiming spirit" of possessiveness, or having sex with too many people or too few or the wrong people in the wrong way. For all of his brave utopianism, John Humphrey Noyes's vision was not in the end about "freeing" love but about regulating and controlling it. Nearly a century after the Oneida community dissolved into bickering and disagreement, the idea of "free love" would remain a proposition far more complicated than it sounds.

By the seventies freedom was beginning to emerge as a terrifying concept, not just to the conservatives who had been objecting to it all along but also to liberals and intellectuals, writers and journalists. Along with the general optimism, the sense of *liberation* and *openness* and *fulfillment*, there developed a critique of the new way of life. It began as certain cynical spectators, like Tom Wolfe, mocked the silliness and idealism of the New Left and the sexual revolution, but it later evolved into a graver and more fashionable pessimism. By 1979, when Joan Didion published her neurasthenic account of the cultural moment, *The White Album*, the apprehension had become widespread. "This sense that it was possible to go 'too far' and that many people were doing it — was very much with us in Los Angeles in 1968 and 1969," Didion wrote. "A demented and seductive vortical tension was building in the community. The jitters were setting in. I recall a time when the dogs barked every night and the moon was always full." There is in this prose an almost biblical apprehension that the end was near. It was a feeling that vast numbers of readers appeared to identify with, a sense of impending doom that seemed to pervade even the most trivial details of their lives. Didion would write about visiting her in-laws and seeing the framed verse "God bless the corners of this house . . .": "This verse had on me the effect of physical chill so insistently did it seem the kind of 'ironic' detail the reporters would seize upon the morning the bodies were found."

If these thoughts seem like the morbid sensitivity of a fragile individual, to Didion's readers it sometimes felt as if the entire country were flowing through her. The radical instability of the times seemed to find its most natural expression in Didion's nervous sensibility. She was giving voice to a paranoid world — where the moon is always full, the dogs are always barking, the bodies about to be found — with a psychological reality all its own. She was picking up on the growing fear that things *were*, in fact, falling apart, the sense of intolerable chaos building to a violent climax.

By the end of the seventies, the jitteriness of Didion's essays had made its way into mainstream movies and novels. In the 1980 Al Pacino movie *Cruising*, two cops drive past Christopher Street in a police car, watching the electric spectacle of tanned, muscular men in jeans and leather jackets cruising each other. One of the cops says, with what now seems like eerie foresight, "Someday this whole city is gonna explode." As guilt turned to panic, the public was suddenly deluged with dark stories of punishment and retribution. The contours of these stories were becoming increasingly familiar: There would be depressing sex scenes in which no one really seemed to like anyone else or even to be particularly *attracted* to them. Someone would consume a lot of drugs. Someone would entertain existential worries about his or her "lifestyle." And then the movie or novel or story would finally end in a spectacular denouement of fire or bloodshed.

There was a pronounced apocalyptic strain to the new plots: People were being killed for their excesses. Moral order was always, in some violent and unpleasant way, restored. John Updike, who had seemed on the whole fairly comfortable with all of the swinging, or at least seemed to think that it made for interesting fiction, himself penned one of the most vivid and disturbing of these new moral parables, *Rabbit Redux*. In its anarchic pages, Rabbit's wife runs off with a Greek car salesman from her father's lot, and Rabbit takes a stray eighteen-year-old into his conventional middle-class suburban home and starts sleeping with her. She becomes a junkie, a dangerous and charismatic black drug dealer moves in, and sexual games of increasing sickness and perversion begin to take over their lives. The story rises to a crescendo of chaos and ends in flames of righteous punishment: Rabbit's house burns down with his doped-up blond mistress inside. His son is traumatized. His wife comes back. And somewhere along the way, Rabbit thinks to himself something that much of the country seemed to have been thinking along with him: *freedom is murder.*

In another popular classic of the period, *Looking for Mr. Goodbar,* freedom literally *is* murder. When the story of a young schoolteacher being stabbed to death by a man she picked up in a singles bar appeared in bookstores in 1975, the country *loved* it. There was something satisfying about the plot, as if this woman's grouchy conservative father had been right all along: she should have stayed home; she should have gotten married. The movie version ends with the memorable scene of her murderer sitting on top of her in bed plunging a knife into her in a grotesque parody of the sex act, while the strobe light freezes the action in oddly sterile purple flashes. The empty pleasure seeking of her life is somehow consummated in her grisly death, and with it the illusions of an entire decade. The cheery search for "growth" and "personal liberation" and "free expression" had ended in the bloody thrust of a knife. And Judith Rossner's unfortunate heroine quickly became a new cultural archetype. The *Philadelphia Inquirer* said that Theresa Dunn "resembles every woman you've ever known." The *Wall Street Journal* wrote, "We know there are Theresa Dunns in our lives, in our offices."

Looking for Mr. Goodbar was one of those novels that seemed to many Americans to speak to their own personal experience, not because there actually *were* lots of Theresa Dunns sipping gin and tonics with homicidal lunatics in bars across the country, but because of a darker and more irrational sense that there *should* be. The sensationalistic story seemed to many people to contain a kind of harsh realism that can only be explained by the guilt and fear lurking right beneath the surface. This fairly average young woman's way of life had never been entirely acceptable, and by this time the whole country seemed, in some sense, to be waiting for Mr. Goodbar.

It was amidst this general atmosphere of anxiety and apprehension that most of us now in our twenties and early thirties spent our childhoods. There was no biological threat to which we could attach our vague premonitions of disaster, no herpes, no AIDS, no uproar about date rape, no reason we needed a "new era of caution and restraint," just an increasing sense that things were reaching a crisis. I remember taking a bright yellow paperback of *Looking for Mr. Goodbar* from my parents' bookshelf and reading it more than once; I remember being haunted by the image of this naked woman bleeding to death on her bed. I remember also the image of her sitting in the bar, sipping her white wine, pretending to read a book, and waiting to pick up a strange man, an image strangely shadowed by my knowledge of what was going to happen to her. Her death seemed somehow natural for an act of random violence. It also seemed to hold some implications about my own life, about the men, bars, wine, and strangers in my future, that I only dimly understood. I wouldn't have been able to explain the danger I felt, curled up on my parents' chintz couch reading the cheap paperback, but I felt it nonetheless.

In the late seventies my younger sister and I would go up to the top floor of our house and find our older sisters rolling thin joints on some sort of red gadget. We found plastic pill cases and somehow knew what they were. We felt, as we sat in our own childish bedroom, wallpapered in a pattern of pink and green elephants, with the Rolling Stones and Velvet Underground pounding loudly above us and the smell of smoke wafting down, that there was something dark and uncontrollable going on upstairs. We didn't feel *safe.* The neatness and order of the bottom floors of the house did nothing to contain that feeling of danger and excess spilling over. It was a child's fear of the vague sexual menace of adolescence, but it bore a certain resemblance to the feeling contained in houses across the country: something bad was going to happen.

It was just around this time that a book called *The New Celibacy* appeared in the pop psychology sections of bookstores, and a twenty-four-year-old woman in Ohio sat down to fill out her answer to one of the questions in the *Cosmo* sex survey: "I'm beginning to wish there was a law against sex." Things were finally beginning to change.

The sense that something bad was going to come out of all the danger and excess of the sixties and seventies was firmly established in the popular imagination before the first sensational articles about herpes began to appear. When the cover stories began to hit the newsstands in 1981, what was notably missing was the tone of surprise. The calm and certainty of assertions like *Esquire*'s — "there is little doubt that Herpes is the dark underside of the sexual revolution" — gave the news a kind of instant neatness and resolution. It was almost as if the country had been listening to a fairy tale for nearly two decades, and at last we were hearing the moral. By the time the photographs of herpes sufferers had spread across the country, the same magazines that had been so enthusiastic about the "emergence from prudery and hypocrisy" were ready to take it all back. The interpretative mechanisms were in place; the apocalyptic news had, in all but its minute details, already been anticipated; and the news copy was infused with a heightened tone of moral significance. "Not even monogamy guarantees herpes-safe sex: Herpes contracted years ago can emerge from its latent state tomorrow, suddenly furiously infectious," warned *Esquire,* anthropomorphizing the virus to give it the glamour and chill of a horror movie. What had happened "years ago" was coming back to haunt us. The irrational fears of the past decade had suddenly become rational ones.

On NBC's nightly news segment on AIDS, Connie Chung narrated gravely, "We were free, then promiscuous. But free love came at a cost. Now we've begun the long trip back." Her tone was that of inevitability, of simple cause and effect. *Free love came at a cost.* She did not say, as Pat Buchanan did in an almost Shakespearean moment, that "the sexual revolution has begun to devour its children," but that is what she meant. Beneath her bland tone, her carefully made-up face and silk blouse, one could hear the faintest whisper of Thomas Hooker regaling his congregation several centuries ago: "All of the plagues inflicted upon the wicked upon the earth issue from the righteous avenging justice of the lord."

Over the next decade, the mild echoes of puritanism in magazines, newspapers, and television broadcasts would become more and more distinct. "We are paying for our sins," an

Atlanta executive told reporters from *Time* for their story on herpes, and in the climate of the early eighties, this suddenly seemed like a perfectly reasonable way to look at the freedom and disorder of the past several decades. The calls for caution and monogamy that proliferated throughout the eighties and nineties contained within them the vehemence and absolutism of religious judgment. The ambivalence that had been there all along was suddenly released with full moral force. " 'Cool sex' cut off from the emotions and rest of life seems empty, unacceptable and immoral," *Time* declared in 1984. That same year one of the founders of the Esalen Institute, the most prominent institution of "free thinking" and "sexual liberation" during the seventies, wrote a book dramatically titled *The End of Sex.*

The accumulation of ironic details such as this one made itself felt in people's lives. "You shouldn't sleep with *anyone* until you get married," my open and liberated mother told me after I graduated from college, suddenly worried about disease. "Are you crazy?" I asked. But she wasn't. She was just presenting the dangerous world to me in all the vividness and exaggeration with which she had received it. "Caution is in. The one-night stand is on the way out," stated the copy of the *New York Times* she read one morning over coffee. "There is something to be said for a deliberate decision to abstain from sexual activity as a means of completely avoiding the risks of sexual exposure to the AIDS virus," declared the sex researchers Masters and Johnson, who had made their reputations, not so long before, with their therapeutic approach to the orgasm. "There is a growing movement toward secondary virginity," announced Donna Shalala, the secretary of the Department of Health and Human Services. There was in this rhetoric of caution an element of fanaticism, a tinge of almost religious intensity that seemed a lot like the ecstatic pursuit of "fulfillment" and orgasms of ten years earlier.

The excessive embrace of "expression" and "liberation" and "openness" had turned into an excessive embrace of prudence. The new credo was almost the mirror image of that of the sexual revolution: Alex Comfort's popular idea that sex was *never* dangerous seemed to have naturally evolved into the idea that sex was *always* dangerous. "Now No One Is Safe from AIDS," warned the cover of *Life*. And this belief that *no one* was safe, and that *nothing* one could do short of never kissing or touching another human being could really protect you, and that *no one* was really to be trusted, was the paranoid vision emerging from posters, magazines, movies, talk shows, and commercials. We were inundated with the idea that, as teachers would phrase it to elementary school students across the country, *there is no such thing as safe sex.*

By the late eighties it became clear that the language of the "new era of caution and restraint" was no more restrained than the language of the sexual revolution. The sweeping apocalyptic feel of titles like *The End of Sex* had a perversely seductive power: the sense of finality itself seemed to have generated a certain amount of excitement. It may have been the "end of sex," this way of thinking went, but it was the beginning of something better. The need for protection became as glorious and celebrated a cause as the need for liberation twenty years earlier. We ended up with pretty sixteen-year-old girls saying things like "It's just not worth risking your whole life for one hour of hoopla" and stores like Condomania declaring, "We are proud to have started a condom revolution!" and school curricula declaring virginity "the true option of sexual freedom." The pursuit of caution had taken on the familiar glow of revolutionary fervor. The *Washington Post* quoted one expert as saying that AIDS might create "even more freedom" because "people will start focusing on long-term relationships." And in 1994 *Newsweek* declared virginity "even more liberating than sex."

The idea that neither virginity nor sex is "liberating" seems to have occurred to relatively few of the public commentators of the past several decades. The country's swaying from one extreme to another, from paradise to exile, wildness to caution, is a symptom of a larger and more complicated malaise. Throughout its history, America has been involved in a perennial oscillation between extremes of liberation and restraint, especially when it comes to sex. From periods of license, such as the Gilded Age of the late 1800s, the 1920s, and the 1970s, we have gone to periods of regulation and restraint, such as the turn of the century, the 1950s, and the 1980s. We have been either wildly enthusiastic about sex, liquor, and cigarettes or completely alarmed by them. They have been symbols of freedom and daring, as they were in Dorothy Parker's time, or they have been symbols of chaos and decline, as they are in ours. The century has witnessed a peculiarly American alternation between an insipid therapeutic search for sexual "fulfillment" and the rigid moralism that is its natural opposite; sex is either sin or salvation.

From the sexual salvation of the sixties, we have emerged into a time when sexual license is taking on the shadowy implications of sin. "Confine your choice of dates," warned *Ebony*'s article on the dangers of disease, "to persons who in your opinion are likely prospects for a stable, monogamous relationship." It might seem to the casual observer that the question of whether or not a relationship is *stable* is only very tangentially related to the question of disease. But by the mid-eighties the word "stability" began cropping up everywhere, as if it were the lack of stability itself that had been the problem. Suddenly all forms of excess and instability seemed to threaten us with disease, which is how we came to have public health pamphlets warning us that "sex under the influence of alcohol or drugs, like driving under the influence, is not safe," which doesn't seem categorically true, and government-funded public service announcements that repeat the broader instruction *"Stay in control, stay in control, stay in control"* as if it were the mantra of a better society. The loss of control, the consumption of a few glasses of wine on a date, the introduction of any degree of "instability," any lack of "commitment," any departure from "monogamy," suddenly seemed, to the keepers of public health and to a certain segment of the public itself, to be tantamount to suicide.

The sexual revolution and the "new era of caution" presented the country with new ideals of sexual behavior, both of which have often been called "healthy" but neither of which, in the more robust sense of the word, actually are. I have a friend whose parents went to a psychologist in the seventies. The psychologist told them that the "healthy" thing to do was to fulfill themselves and follow their own desires. They got divorced because, in the late summer of 1973, that was somehow what they were *supposed* to do. Although this interpretation may be from the skewed perspective of a five-year-old child watching his parents run off with their respective lovers like the naked illustrations in *The Joy of Sex,* there *was* an element of danger and destructiveness to all the "liberation" that was in the air. As my friend tells it, there was something naive and depressing about his parents' belief that "sexual expression" and "sexual fulfillment" could actually save them. But equally depressing and untrue is the growing belief that *not* having sex is somehow going to save us. The inflated rhetoric of caution is just as deceptive and finally as irrelevant as the official platitudes of the sexual revolution. As alarming as any of the long-haired visionaries of the sixties are the typical Americans emerging from the current articles in *Time* and *Newsweek* who stay home and rent videos, and eat fat-free ice cream, and use the Stairmaster 3.5 times a week at the gym, never have more than one drink, and never feel the rush of unexpected intimacy coursing, dark and heavenly, through their veins.

The Selling of Caution

It's Sunday night, and I'm stretching out lazily on my couch as a woman in a satin ball gown and a man in a tuxedo waltz across my television screen. A rich voice purrs, "If you've had sex with two people, and each of *those* two people has had sex with two people, and each of *those* two people has had sex with two people . . ." The ballroom fills with identical couples, giving the advertisement the feel and texture of a nightmare, and forcing me, along with the 19.4 million other viewers, into an uneasy contemplation of my own romantic history. "For more information call 1-800-342-AIDS."

I am part of the demographic this public service announcement is designed to reach, and I am susceptible to its peculiarly mathematical formulation of a fundamentally emotional fear: *it's wrong to have so many intimate relationships.* Have I slept with too many people? I start thinking back. I consider making a list.

According to the new set of messages promoting sexual caution, we've all slept with too many people. As the ballroom and the waltzing couples dissolve into blackness, it occurs to me that these advertisements may capture for later generations the distinctive anxiety of the times: the warnings of sexual danger that fill our television screens will appear in the history books of the future as illustrations of our disenchantment with the ideals of sexual consumption. In its echoes our descendants will hear our fatigue; in the identical couples popping up across the screen, they will see our fear of anonymity, of not mattering to the person we are with; they will find in them visual evidence of our exhaustion with our own version of fin de siècle decadence.

The ballroom advertisement and others like it originated with the arresting and frequently quoted safe sex slogan "You are sleeping with everyone your partner has ever slept with," launched by Dr. Otis R. Bowen, the secretary of Health and Human Services under President Ronald Reagan. "When a person has sex, they're not just having it with that partner," he said in a press conference in 1987. "They're having it with everybody that partner has had it with for the past ten years." And somehow his clunky phrase remained impressed in our minds as a convincing formulation of the warning, a warning that in its odd bureaucratic language seemed to speak to our deeper sense that everyone was sleeping with everyone, that the sexual disorder of the past several decades was reaching an intolerable threshold. The phrase cropped up in classrooms and advertisements, in *Time* and *Newsweek*, and on television shows like *L.A. Law*. It was quoted casually as a fact at cocktail parties, restaurants, and college dining halls. And before long it began to seem like the most natural way in the world to think about relationships.

If the deceptively simple slogan "You are sleeping with

everyone your partner has ever slept with" seemed at first like a convenient way of translating the epidemiology of the disease into the popular imagination, it also proposed a new ideal of sexual behavior, which involves the somewhat unlikely proposition that neither you nor your partner has ever slept with anyone else. By this new calculus, every sexual act becomes promiscuous; every sexual act becomes perverse. The slogan is so luridly literal that it practically demands that you visualize all your past sexual partners in one place, and in so doing it evokes the chaos and confusion of a certain style of life: it reminds you how many people you've been close to, how many dates you've been on, how many beds you've woken up in, how many relationships you've begun and ended. In its absoluteness, the slogan betrays a certain fanaticism. Everyone is implicated; no one is innocent.

Dr. Bowen's phrase also inspired a particularly creative line of safe sex videos in which a couple kiss and all their old boyfriends and girlfriends appear magically in bed with them. Each time I've seen one of these videos, the audience laughs as the past sexual partners are conjured up amidst pillows and comforters, but in the appreciative laughter is a slightly nervous strain — a knowledge that in the simple absurdity and theatricality of the image, there is also a kind of psychological realism. These videos are playing on the eerie sense that we are not really alone with the person we think we're alone with, that each intimate moment is shadowed by past intimate moments, that the fast and fluid nature of modern relationships reduces us all to notches on each other's belts, names on a list, a faceless blur of affection.

The first time I saw one of these videos, I realized that

this is, in some complicated emotional sense, an accurate picture of the way I am living my life, and the way most people I know are also: amidst the letters, books, sweaters, photographs, answering machine messages, and other accumulated clutter of past relationships. What is so haunting about slogans like "You are sleeping with everyone your partner has ever slept with" is that they violate all the traditional images of love and romantic specialness that are engraved in silver letters on Hallmark cards: "You are my true love," "We were made for each other," "You are the only one." Instead they present us with the opposite idea: you are only one among many.

I remember finding a shoe box of letters that a boyfriend had received from a previous girlfriend in Italy. I remember reading the words "I love you" scrawled in blue ink at the bottom of each page of creamy stationery and thinking about how many women had written the same words to him and how impersonal the words become when you say them over and over again to different people. It suddenly hit me — the sense of my own letters occupying only one shoe box in my boyfriend's emotions. Of course this particular form of jealousy is not unique to our time and place. W. H. Auden wrote in 1939 that every man and woman craves precisely what they cannot have: "Not universal love / But to be loved alone." But there is something in our current circumstances, in people marrying later and having more intimate relationships with more people, that seems to draw attention to just how impossible it is "to be loved alone."

The feeling of desperation that suffuses safe sex advertisements and videos becomes a moral commentary on the way that we've been living for the past several decades, which is why, sitting in front of them, my own fairly average romantic history seems impossibly sordid and why nearly everyone watching them feels similarly judged. What we are really seeing projected across our television screens in advertisements, safe sex videos, after-school specials, and talk shows is the refraction of a larger social apprehension: about the rise in divorce rates and the delaying of the marriage age and about how our culture has come to seem almost *designed* to accommodate a series of shifting emotional attachments.

To take one of the most visible illustrations of how relationships have been affected by the cultural shifts of the past few decades, the demographics of marriage have changed substantially. According to the U.S. Census Bureau's latest statistics, the median marriage age jumped from twenty for women and twenty-three for men in 1964 to twenty-five for women and twenty-seven for men in 1994. A glance through the wedding section of the *New York Times* reveals that for urban professionals, the marriage age is significantly higher. Now that it's perfectly normal for people to marry in their thirties, relationships are conducted in a new spirit of transience and fluidity, of sampling and testing.

We have a picture that goes along with the simpler conception of romantic destiny: a very young bride and groom who glide smiling and smooth-faced to the altar like the flawless plastic figures on a wedding cake. But what emerges more perplexingly from the census figures is a bemused, slightly older couple who have decided to get married after other relationships haven't worked out, after living with people and moving out, after dividing posters and books, after countless dinners and flings and affairs. For that couple the vows have a different resonance. Contained within them, now more than ever, is the knowledge of the vows one could have taken but didn't, the might-have-beens. Our traditional conceptions of love are more suited to a time when college seniors at Vassar, Smith, and Wellesley felt compelled to get a "ring before spring" and when couples generally tended to get married before they had sex with enough people to fill a ballroom.

An Australian advertisement, which has many American counterparts, gives this anxiety — "You are only one among many" — a striking physical embodiment. A couple giggles in bed together under a blue wool blanket, with their feet sticking out, in a kind of harmless fantasy of domesticity that lulls us into a warm sense of security. Then the camera draws back, and we see the couple in a factory-like environment with thousands of other naked couples in rows and rows of identical beds, mechanically reaching for each other beneath identical sky blue blankets. This alarming and, on the purely literal level, absurd image seems almost calculated to create a physical revulsion in the viewer. "You never know," a voice warns, "exactly how many people you are going to bed with." As the camera rolls through the rows of beds, our sense of tranquillity vanishes, and we are drawn into an atmosphere of sexual panic: the roomful of beds feels somehow familiar, like somewhere we've been before.

The identical couples reflect our worst fears about our own lives: that our affections and those of the people we're with are as random and interchangeable as the camera mischievously suggests, that the accumulation of romantic experiences lends a kind of generic quality to the most intimate attachments. The visual power of the identical beds lifts the advertisement above its surface content: "You never know exactly how many people you are going to bed with" takes on broad and spooky moral overtones. It becomes an argument against impersonal sex. If there had never been a fatal sexually transmitted disease, the image of sleeping with someone in a roomful of other couples would inspire a similar fear, a fear that is not at its heart about physical health, but about what our relationships can possibly mean in a world with this kind of emotional landscape. The identical beds seem to tell us, *You think you're special, but you're not.*

These advertisements are not just about disease; they are also about a state of mind. A thirty-year-old friend tells me about meeting his new girlfriend's parents. "I just couldn't summon up the energy to be charming. I've done it so many times before," he said. His confession startled me. It was one of those things that you are just not supposed to say. I knew what he meant, though. He was having trouble summoning up the requisite romantic hopefulness because he had already been through so many relationships. It's as if he experienced, as he ate veal and wine with this woman's parents in a French restaurant, a sudden awareness of the rows of identical beds furnishing his past. He had trouble saying to himself, *This is it.*

In a culture where 70 to 80 percent of teenagers have sex and most don't get married until their mid- to late twenties, these sorts of patterns, repetitions, and echoes may be inevitable. I once went out with a man who told me that he had slept with five Katies, and I felt as he said it a similar chill. The fact is that the traditional vocabulary of romantic destiny no longer speaks to most of our romantic experiences, which involve precisely this type of multiplicity, this division, this replication. The images of the crowd touch on the secret nightmare of a generation: if you've slept with a lot of people, lived with a few, and dated countless others, how can you really believe that anyone is "the only one"?

As the ballroom advertisement flickered across my television screen, it seemed to provide a definitive replacement for the fading values of the sixties and seventies, when the whole culture toyed with the idea of slipping from bed to bed, of being free of the constraints of monogamy, fidelity, and remaining chaste until marriage. Bestselling guides to life in the early seventies actually included sentences like "As people, we must flow with life and its changes." In fact that whole seventies language about "swinging" and being "free," about not being "tied down" and "hung up," involved a lack of accountability, a flowing through things, and it is precisely this type of movement that is revealed to be impossible: the past, according to this new set of messages, is inescapable. These advertisements present instead a radical vision of the responsibility that appeared to have evaporated during the seventies: every tiny little thing will come back to haunt you. As we watch the couples multiplying across the screen, we see the whole dream of the sexual revolution take on the nervous tones of a nightmare.

Every culture has its own way of representing the threat of sexually transmitted disease and putting it out on the airwaves and television screens of the nation's consciousness. In Canada a middle-age couple in tight sweaters and plaid pants primly declare, "It is our commitment to each other that protects us from AIDS." In France the warnings tend to resemble breath-less sex scenes, in which the camera zooms in on bare breasts and condoms sensuously unwrapped.

One bright, windy day in November 1995, members of the press showed their photo identification in the hushed lobby of the Department of Health and Human Services to wit-ness the unveiling of the U.S. government's latest campaign of public service announcements about AIDS: "Protect Your-self, Respect Yourself." This campaign is, in the words of one reporter, less "flowery and nebulous" than the government's previous efforts. He may have been thinking of the Bush era advertisement in which a man pulling on a sock was meant to symbolize to the chaste nation the use of a condom. The new advertisements are, for the most part, direct and to the point, although the point itself occasionally strays from what are con-ventionally considered issues of public health into the territory traditionally covered in women's magazines and evangelical sermons.

Lydia Ogden, a spokesperson for the Centers for Disease Control, tells me firmly, "We are *not* in the moral arbitration business." But many of the advertisements that the reporters are craning to see on the small television screen at the front of the room seem to be motivated by precisely that. In spite of the slick MTV graphics, the scrawling purple graffiti, and the fashionably distorted images, the perspective of these par-ticular advertisements often seems to come from a distinctively pre-MTV era. A pretty black girl in a red college sweatshirt stares wide-eyed at the audience: "I don't understand my girl-friends. They say, 'I'm in love,' and it's a different guy every three weeks." What she is talking about is the flimsiness of attachments, the fast, transitory emotions of pop song lyrics, not the threat of sexually transmitted disease. "My aunts are my role models," she continues. "They didn't have sex until they were *married*." A blond girl appears on the screen, her eyes caked with blue mascara and eyeliner. "Secondary virginity is what I practice," she says, sounding a little like one of those dolls that talk when you pull the string. "Next time I have sex will be when I'm *married*." These words appear on the screen: "Respect yourself, protect yourself. Call the national AIDS hotline. . . ."

These advertisements involve a more ambitious view of social change than simply whipping an apathetic population into a state of sufficient anxiety that they go out and buy boxes of Trojans from the local drugstore. What we are hearing is the voice of fifties morality with a slightly defensive edge, as the wisdom of that period masquerades as a reasonable health precaution. "This is our vision for the future," Donna Shalala, the tiny secretary of health and human services, says proudly from the podium. The audience is buoyed for a moment by her tone of hopefulness and optimism, until we realize, shifting uncomfortably in our plastic seats, that there is something sort of eerie about this vision of the future, a vision that seems, in fact, to come directly out of the past. It starts to get depressing, watching all of these beaming, well-adjusted kids looking out at us through the rich hues of color television and telling us that they've decided not to have sex.

On the subject of what exactly they are trying to accomplish, the spokespeople for the Centers for Disease Control and the Department of Health and Human Services tend to sound as confused as the rest of us. One spokeswoman tells me, "We know that a ten-second ad doesn't change anyone's personal experience, but we are trying to change cultural norms." Another spokeswoman tells me, "We are *not* trying to change social norms. We are trying to reinforce healthy norms." Whatever it is that they are or are not trying to do to the country's norms, the word "healthy," in this context, is not an entirely physical concept.

"We have seen promising signs of a greater degree of sexual abstinence among young people," Donna Shalala drones on from the podium, "and a growing movement toward secondary virginity." Shalala's wording seems out of place in the neutral bureaucratic setting — the plush gray velvet curtains behind her, the American flag hanging dutifully next to the podium, the Department of Health and Human Services emblems plastered all over everything — but the sheer strangeness of her utterance seems lost on most of the gathered reporters who take it all down. I start to write the words into my notebook and then I stop. *Secondary virginity?* Only in America would people believe that they could reinvent themselves as virgins, and only in America would a high-placed public official speak respectfully of those people.

The authenticity of the government's ads is so vehemently established by the constant reiteration that they feature "real young people" and were approved by a committee of "real young people" that one begins to wonder what there is about them not to believe. They have a shimmer of artificiality, a sheen of propaganda, that the realness of the young people, the roughness of the camera angles, and the sensibleness of much of their message do nothing to undermine. As one of the reporters said to me afterward, you can't quite shake the feeling that you are being *sold* something, like a shiny new Honda Civic.

What these ads are selling us is a more monogamous, virtuous version of ourselves. In one of the previous campaign's "I want to spend my life with you" segments, a woman gazes dreamily into the camera, lips parted suggestively, and says in a throaty voice over the elevator music being piped into the background, "I want you. I want to spend my life with you. . . . I'll never hurt you, never lie to you, and never put you in danger. There is a time for us to be lovers. We will wait until that time." And then the words "America Responds to AIDS" appear on the screen. Here again one can't help thinking that one is witnessing America responding to more than simply the appearance of the AIDS virus. The United States government seems to be suggesting to its citizens a more permanent, long-range view of relationships. We are receiving, through the airwaves and television satellites, the homespun advice from thirty years ago: don't sleep with anyone until you hear the words "I want to spend my life with you."

Where is this advice coming from? It is tempting to imagine a bureaucrat in a small room at the top of the Department of Health and Human Services designing these advertisements to control the libido of the nation spread out beneath his window in the gray Washington streets dotted with tiny cars. But there was, in fact, a tremendous amount of research behind the creation of the new campaign. The ads are based on "mall intercepts" and "continuous response technology," in which a large number of people were taken from the malls of America, where they were browsing through sneakers and miniskirts, and electronically monitored to see which segments triggered the deepest response. As Lydia Ogden of the Centers for Disease Control explains the careful, scientific process by which these ads are produced, one begins to get the sense that we are receiving the brain waves of the country, that these ads are electronically telegraphing our nation's deepest beliefs and fears. There seems to be some transcendent truth in the words of the pretty black girl — "I don't regret not having sex; I know I'm better off" — that has less to do with the psychological reality of virginity than with the collective fantasy of sixteen-year-olds so world-weary that they would like to reinvent themselves as virgins and a nation that would, on some level, like to imagine itself pure again.

Behind the safe sex campaigns of the nineties are the same moral concerns more obviously invested in the campaign against syphilis nearly half a century ago: the posters of the whole family gathered around a smiling housewife in an apron, icing a cake in her kitchen, with the unambiguous words, "Go back to them physically fit and morally clean." In the language of advertisements, television news broadcasts, and magazines, the danger has subtly become not a disease but a "lifestyle." It's a commonplace that everyone from left-wing activists such as Larry Kramer to *Time* magazine to Pat Buchanan uses in conjunction with the disease. Magic Johnson announced that he got AIDS from his "Hollywood lifestyle," Tommy Morrison got it from his "promiscuous lifestyle," and others are said to have gotten it from their "fast lifestyle" or their "carefree lifestyle." Out of the jumbled collage of images, quotations, and posters, we receive the impression that we should not just try to use condoms but that our "lifestyle" itself has to change.

From the beginning, the idea of selling caution to the country has involved more than simply passing on information. As Adam Glickman, the president and founder of Condomania, explained, "We need a whole philosophy of safer sex," and the "whole philosophy" that's being sketched out in classrooms, condom stores, subway posters, magazines, movies, and advertisements involves not only the necessity of using condoms but also other pressing issues of public health, like "stable, monogamous relationships," "love," "commitment," "communication," "abstinence," and "rethinking our values."

When I first walk into Condomania, I am immediately enveloped in its atmosphere of cheerfulness, peppiness, and clean all-American fun. One of the walls is covered with condoms blown up like elongated balloons at a child's birthday party. This is the environment that most clearly embodies the new philosophy of "safer sex." There are candy jars filled with condoms and an eager-to-please staff who brightly ask blushing customers every ten seconds, "Can I help you with anything?" With condom T-shirts and boxer shorts covering every available inch of wall space, the store looks almost like a tourist attraction, where Mom and Pop can buy pet condoms and fake plants with bright condom blossoms and other kitschy items for Aunt Sylvia back home.

As I browse through the store, I begin having paranoid thoughts about my romantic past. I think about all the condoms I *haven't* used. "Can I give you any advice?" the salesman asks gently, giving me a meaningful look, and I start getting nervous. "No thanks, I'm just looking," I say, and I become increasingly focused on the microthin, ultrasleek ribbed condoms hanging on the wall in front of me. The sheer variety of condoms, the abundance and choice, suggest the excess of caution and perpetual edginess that are part of the whole phenomenon of safe sex. The concept provokes a kind of nagging insecurity: *Do I have enough of them? Do I have the right kind? Will this kind work, or will that kind work better?*

Of course this is in part a commercial trick — to convince the consumer of some glaring need or absence in their life waiting to be filled — but it is also part of the "whole philosophy" Glickman was talking about, which involves the sneaking suspicion that nothing you do will ever *completely* protect you. In fact, one of the strangest and most revealing features of the attempt to sell sexual caution to the country is the conviction that you can never really be cautious enough. People on the Right and on the Left, health educators, condom sales representatives, and religious fundamentalists, all agree that "there is no such thing as safe sex." "Don't ever use the word *safe*," Glickman warned me. "The correct way to say it is *safer* sex."

This conservative approach to safety applies to how we are supposed to think about our actions as well as our vocabulary. On their brand-new Web site, for instance, Condomania lists "French-kissing" under the not very reassuring heading "Somewhat Safe Behaviors." *Somewhat safe.* This vision of the dangers of the French kiss does not come out of any scientific evidence — the Centers for Disease Control have no documented cases of HIV transmitted through kissing of any kind — nor does it appear to emerge out of any obvious commercial motives. (According to a *New York Times* article on the prudence of showing French kissing on television, one of the networks appears to share Condomania's view on the subject: "According to Thomas Kersey, vice president of broadcasting,

ABC's policies already forbid open-mouthed kissing. 'We advise our producers that the French kiss is unacceptable,' he said. 'If we see a tongue flashing we will edit it out.' ") It's not that French-kissing puts you at any measurable risk for disease but that the *state of mind* in which French-kissing is only "somewhat safe" is somehow considered desirable.

Behind all the exhortations to be safe is the idea that safety is impossible. The whole philosophy of "safer sex" involves a kind of perpetual anxiety. Even if you follow every precaution, it tells us, there is no way to protect yourself. That the word "safe" is such a taboo, that it seems so extreme a guarantee, so unattainable a goal that it forever eludes our grasp, reveals that the word is operating on a not entirely literal level. It reveals the almost magical function of the concept: no matter what you do, no matter which of the dazzling array of rainbow-colored latex options you choose, what is threatening to you — and to all of us — is that you are having sex at all.

The condom lollipops and condom candy jars, the cuteness and innocence of it all, the transparent aquas, pinks, and purples, give you the distinct sense that you are buying a pretty-colored, attractively packaged thing that just *happens* to be a condom. On the walls are a whole line of euphemistically named products like finger condoms ("safe touch") and latex gloves ("love gloves") and bright green dental dams, which Don Francis, one of the leading AIDS experts in the country, has called "expensive and really silly" and which even Adam Glickman refers to as "safer sex for the absolutely paranoid." In the extremes to which the concept of safety is taken, in the products like "love gloves" and "safe touch," in the imaginative lengths to which we are willing to go, we can see the ideology at work: the deeply held conviction that we can never really be safe. The paranoia lays bare the puritanical belief that there are dark and uncontrollable forces contained in the sexual impulse itself.

I remember reading a short story about an attractive lawyer who wanted her boyfriend to wear an entire suit of saran wrap to keep their bodies from touching, and it does feel as if that's where this new "philosophy" is heading: to a fastidiousness so extreme that it leads to a clinical suspicion of everyone else. If you spend enough time in Condomania, you really do begin to fantasize about a body wrapped in saran wrap, a vision of absolute protection, that defies all logic, all medical facts, and becomes a kind of metaphor for all the risks of contact itself. The only way out of the danger is through complete isolation. For $1.50 you can buy a mint-flavored condom, for $1.25 you can get ten finger condoms, and for $3.25 you can get a bag of three dental dams. But they seem strangely beside the point. There is a level of security that you can't buy over the counter.

Sentimental Education

The people most relentlessly and aggressively being sold the idea of caution in this country are teenagers like the ones at Parsippany Hills High School in northern New Jersey. They don't talk about "birth control," which sounds strange and old-fashioned to them; they talk about "protected" and "unprotected" sex. Most of them are still having it, but with the particular sense of heightened drama, of raised stakes that has been impressed on them by teachers, parents, and cartoon condoms scampering across their television screens at one in the morning. It's a measure of how quickly and completely things have changed that they don't find it odd sitting through classes on masturbation or learning about the eternal mysteries of sex underneath a black-and-white poster of blobs of infected cells seen through a microscope with the slogan "Sleep around and you could wind up with more than a good time." They take it all for granted. The equation sex can equal death has been chalked into their minds along with the multiplication tables.

"OK, you guys," says Carole Adamsbaum, a heavy woman

in a flowing orange sleeveless dress with a white T-shirt underneath in the style of *Seventeen* magazine.

These kids look really young. They may be freshmen in high school, but they have the bewildered expression of children who woke up one morning in the wrong bodies — suddenly finding themselves either too tall or too thin or too plump. Slamming their notebooks onto their desks and settling into their seats with a kind of showy reluctance, they keep moving until the last possible moment, squirming, turning to each other, taking things out of their purses, rattling their pencils, tapping their carefully chosen sneakers against the chairs in front of them, basically exuding the sense that they are here against their will. They don't look as if they could possibly be having sex, but then, as they themselves tell me afterward, looks can be deceiving.

"How does AIDS affect your lives?" Carole Adamsbaum begins, her thick glasses magnifying her warm, chocolate brown eyes. "Let's go around the room."

"I'm going to be careful about who I get close with," says a pretty olive-skinned girl in the front row.

"I use condoms," says the boy next to her simply.

"It hasn't affected my life," says a tiny Asian boy in a neat button-down shirt, and then, catching the glint of annoyance that flashes through Ms. Adamsbaum's eyes, he quickly adds, "At least not yet. I'm sure it will."

Even though Adamsbaum's question sounds like an open one, it isn't. The room itself leaves no doubt about the answer. Every available inch of wall space is covered with posters that tell these kids how AIDS is supposed to be affecting their lives: "If you get the AIDS virus now, you and your license might expire at the same time." The words leap out in the same serious black-and-white tones as the photographs beneath them. The threat plastered all over the walls — *If you have sex, you may die* — hangs heavily in the air. "Ever notice how attractive it is to be alive?" asks a generic photo of three smiling girls with their arms around each other. The jingle writers seem to be working on the assumption that death is not a meaningful concept to teenagers. They are trying to translate the danger of AIDS into the world of fast cars, sports, and Saturday nights.

As Ms. Adamsbaum goes around the room, most of the fifteen-year-olds answer her simply and openly. They want to do well. They want to give the right answers. But a few of them are sullen, withholding. They coolly project a kind of physical absence. When Ms. Adamsbaum speaks to them, their bodies tense with resistance, and they speak in the short, hostile monosyllables of adolescent protest. They are trying to keep some part of themselves secret.

"Does AIDS affect *you?*" Ms. Adamsbaum asks one of the sullen types.

"Nah," he says. He is sitting right beneath an "I ♡ Whales" poster.

"Are you going to use condoms?" she asks, just a hint of warning edging into her voice.

"I don't know," he says finally, and the class is quiet with tension. Openness is encouraged in this classroom, but there are still right and wrong answers.

"I am," a confident black male voice calls out finally from the back row. "I don't trust no one. Not even my wife when I get one. She could be playing around."

"Do you think AIDS might make you wait a while to have sex?" Adamsbaum asks him.

"Yeah," he says, considering. "I guess."

After that the class reviews — and the glazed expressions on these kids' faces give new meaning to the word "review" — the behaviors that would put them at risk for AIDS. With an air of having been over this a million times, one girl answers finally, "Sex."

"Be more specific," prods Ms. Adamsbaum. "I count holding hands as sex."

A boy passes a note to a fragile-looking girl with Botticelli curls and pale blue eyes heavily ringed with black eye makeup. She giggles.

What we teach these kids about sex probably doesn't get through their narrow-eyed, gum-chewing cool. It seems to me that whatever we teach them, chances are they'll do what generations have done before them — hearts beating faster, hands faltering, pants crinkling beneath sneakers, mouths tasting of beer. Some of them will remember the condoms in their pockets, and some of them won't. But in these classes we are seeing something else at work: our cultural anxieties about sex, our ambivalence, our awkward attempts to find some new technical, institutional code to replace the power of old-fashioned morality.

"Moral and religious codes have been weak and helpless in determining an influence over sexual conduct," wrote Margaret Sanger in her passionate book on anatomy and venereal diseases, *What Every Boy and Girl Should Know*. In arguing the importance of "sex instruction" in 1927, Margaret Sanger was making the same kind of practical argument that sex educators make today: moral and religious taboos weren't stopping young people from "taking sex like a cocktail," as D. H. Lawrence put it, but maybe the horror of syphilis would. During moments of tremendous social change, like the Jazz Age or the seventies, when young people are zigzagging around with a new sense of freedom and there seems to be a general breakdown of civilized behavior, the prospect of sex education appears to offer a certain amount of order. Margaret Sanger didn't talk about virtue; she talked about "cleanliness." Her idea was to influence the sexual development of young people not with outdated moral prohibitions but with a clearheaded statement of facts. Of course the facts were different then — for instance, Sanger's earnest warnings about the perils ensuing to "chronic masturbators" — but the larger theory was the same: to create a code of sexual ethics out of science.

In a country that wouldn't allow the printing and distribution of *Lady Chatterley's Lover,* however, the idea of frank talks about sexuality in schools met with inevitable and passionate resistance. But sex slowly entered the classroom, and the first sex education film, dryly titled *Human Growth,* titillated students in 1948. Today's sex education, however, has gone beyond the naming of the parts; it's gone beyond the facts of life into the feelings, which is how the kids at Parsippany Hills High School came to have a multiple-choice final exam question on whether "sexuality is the physical expression of oneself."

Carole Adamsbaum wheels over the television screen, which, balanced on a high metal stand, oddly resembles a human form. She dims the lights and turns on an MTV-style video in which attractive young people offer frank advice about AIDS. "Here's the stuff you need to know," the pretty black girl on the screen tells us. Sexual intercourse ("your standard guy-girl form of sex") is risky. Pictures of young couples and drug users whiz by. Loud music plays. Then the scene cuts to three girls in leotards and tights stretching their legs at a ballet bar, giggling and gossiping about a cute boy one of them just met. At first they give a lifelike appearance of intimacy, confusion, banter, and the subtle play of power between girls, but then one of them lapses into the wooden tones of sex education: "If you can't talk to him about condoms, you shouldn't be having sex with him." The kids sit perfectly still and stare at the screen, its purple light dancing across their faces, which look particularly childlike in the dark. This is something they are used to. Use condoms, the video tells them, condoms are cool.

"I look on AIDS as making it easier to get the school districts to talk about sex," Carole Adamsbaum says as we drink watery coffee in the small, brightly colored faculty lounge. The blues and oranges of the tables and chairs add a kind of subdued gaiety to the conversation.

Outside the school, the Toyotas, Lincolns, Plymouths, and Fords glitter in the sun. Their bumper stickers — "Save the Trees," "Sonic Youth," and "Humpty Dumpty Was Pushed" — are like stray thoughts emanating from the concrete walls of the institution. The school newspaper reports a possible "racial incident" in the cafeteria. The kids claim that their lockers are regularly searched for drugs and weapons. An American flag ripples in the wind.

Carole Adamsbaum has been involved in sex education since the early days of the state of New Jersey's mandate for sex education in the late seventies. Since then AIDS has given everyone, on the Right and on the Left, a new sense of urgency, or rather a new excuse for their sense of urgency. It's given the sexual debates a tangible raison d'être: on the Left because now we *have* to teach teenagers about condoms, and on the Right because now we *have* to teach teenagers not to have sex. I once read somewhere that one of the results of the AIDS virus was that newscasters have to say the words "anal sex" on television. Sex education is affected by the same principle of being scared into a kind of increased explicitness. AIDS has given everyone a reason to lobby harder and shout louder: it has thrust sexual morality into the news.

"I know AIDS isn't spreading into the mainstream hetero-sexual community at the rates they originally predicted," Ms. Adamsbaum continues. "But I don't want the kids to know that. I don't want them to relax too much. I'd rather they were scared."

This seems to be a relatively common calculation. "I think teachers and adults are very scared to be totally honest with kids," says Susan Wilson, the head of New Jersey Network for Family Life Education, an organization that trains teachers and analyzes and promotes the state's sex education programs. "We say that we're all at risk. The reality is that if you're poor, if you're black, if you're from the inner city where the disease is rife, you're at much greater risk than if you're living in the suburbs."

Carole Adamsbaum's decision to deliberately exaggerate the risk of AIDS is a reasonable one. Better safe than sorry. It's hard enough to get teenagers, with their crazy moods and hor-mones, their consumption of great quantities of beer and pot and vodka stolen from their parents' liquor cabinets, and their usual delusions of immortality, to be careful. If a slight overstatement of the danger protects even one of these kids, it's worth it. But Ms. Adamsbaum's admission nonetheless adds a gloss of propaganda: she is telling these kids what she thinks they should hear, not what she thinks is true.

This large woman with her warm smile and her thick Brooklyn accent brings an odd assortment of attitudes to her teaching: a shy maternal protectiveness mingled with a sort of salacious encouragement. "Some people say that I am turning the kids on to sexual intercourse. I hope I'm not doing that. I don't want to do that." She pauses, with a definite grasp of the dramatic potential of her role. "I want to turn them on to masturbation."

Carole Adamsbaum talks about her work with the defiant pride of a porn star. She knows that there are people all over America who would picket outside the modern concrete-and-glass structure of Parsippany Hills High School if they knew what was going on in Room B-26. Even though most of the parents in the community support what she is doing, she knows that her position is not entirely secure. She had to make dozens of phone calls to keep a woman who is hostile toward her teaching philosophy from being elected to the school board. "So far I've been lucky," she says, her big brown eyes shining with a sense of urgency about her mission, which is to bring safe and guilt-free sexuality to the children of suburban New Jersey.

"I make no secret of it," Carole Adamsbaum says, her face crinkling into a mischievous smile. "I'm a big fan of masturbation." Then she takes me to a class on that subject taught by a student teacher.

*   *   *

"Why do people masturbate?" the pale, sandy-haired teacher asks.

The class is silent.

"For pleasure?" she asks, a nervous smile fluttering hopefully over her small, birdlike features.

"So they don't get diseases or pregnant," offers one girl good-naturedly.

"I saw something on *Oprah* about this," says a plump girl in a midriff-baring T-shirt as she chews her pink Bubble Yum. "This woman said that when she masturbated, her migraine headaches went away."

"Right," beams the birdlike teacher. "Masturbation relieves tension."

The kids don't giggle. They don't look uncomfortable. If anything, they look sort of blasé. This could be algebra class for all they care, $A = \pi r^2$ being written on the board while they chew their gum and doodle elaborate logos and designs in the margins of their notebooks. If there is any sign of nervousness at all, it is the legs bouncing restlessly beneath the desks.

We've certainly come a long way from the days when Margaret Sanger wrote to her young readers, "The important thing to remember is that masturbation can be conquered." But what exactly is being taught in this class? These kids are not being given any physical details. The thin, sandy-haired teacher in her prim cotton dress doesn't show them how to masturbate, as she might in the tossing nightmares of the Christian Right. She doesn't give them any special how-to tips or hand out copies of *Penthouse* to take home as study aids. She does tell them that the nineteenth-century myths about masturbation — that it makes you go blind, that it makes hair grow on your hands — are not true. But somehow I don't think that these children of the late twentieth century are really staying up late worrying about going blind from touching themselves. The point of the class is actually much more general — it is simply the act of talking about masturbation in the classroom that matters. It's a display of openness. Nothing is really being learned or taught; it is the sheer repetition of the word that matters: masturbation becomes an officially acceptable, school-sanctioned activity.

Altogether, sex education seems to have less to do with education than it might appear. The object of all of these health classes is not simply the dissemination of information. With information about sex so available and so detailed, by the time a third- or fourth- or fifth-grade class sits down to talk about sex, chances are the kids have stared at a tattered page of *Playboy*, watched *Basic Instinct,* or read an article in *Cosmopolitan* on "what he really wants in bed" or how to make condoms fun. Chances are they've pieced together some reasonably accurate picture of the sexual act. These kids watch television. They read magazines. They know about condoms. They know about AIDS. "I've known about condoms for about ten years," sighs a fifteen-year-old, tossing her coppery perm on her way out of class. And even for those who have managed to make it through all those years without absorbing this information, the physical techniques of condom use hardly require an entire curriculum. But it's not the facts themselves that matter; it's the task of guiding and shaping the teenage sensibility. The idea is that there has to be a voice of authority: a disembodied, teacherly voice that enters their messy bedrooms, their parents' cars, the dark grassy fields under the stars, and whispers in their ears.

In all of the debates about sex education, we aren't really arguing over whether or not to use words such as "masturbation" and "condoms" in the classroom but over something more elusive and more important: a shared cultural position on sex. The fierce moral struggle takes strangely literal, and sometimes seemingly trivial, forms. In the state of New Jersey, it was a battle between those who wanted a "stress abstinence" bill requiring that teachers stick to a "just say no" approach to be passed through the state legislature and those who opposed it. In other districts, the struggle takes other forms — a fight over a teacher, over an abstinence curriculum like the controversial "Sex Respect" package that teaches kids to save themselves until marriage, or over handing out condoms or talking about masturbation. The ill-fated, much-mocked former surgeon general Joycelyn Elders famously said, "Everyone in the world is opposed to sex outside of marriage, and yet everybody does it. I'm saying, *Get real*." And so there are the moralists, who are trying to protect the innocence of the very young, and the realists, who don't believe in it. The simple, passionate format of this debate conceals an atmosphere of moral confusion, a profound uncertainty about what on earth we should be teaching our children.

In the reassuring pages of Jane Austen novels, there are clear lines of propriety telling you not to ride alone in open carriages with young men, not to go to balls without the chaperoning presence of a married woman, and not to fall in love with someone beneath you in social class. In the fifties, there were curfews on college campuses and social taboos against getting a "bad reputation" or losing your virginity before you got married. But now we have no popularly accepted moral attitude about sexuality that can be passed down from one generation to the next. Is it all right for teenagers to have sex, or isn't it? Is it morally wrong or just physically dangerous? We don't have an answer. It's not just that different people have different answers, but that, for the first time in recent memory, we don't have an official answer, an answer that extends from *Oprah* to Hollywood to the editorial pages of the *New York Times*.

In 1992 we elected a president whose unfaithfulness to his wife was discussed on national television (unlike the infidelities of John F. Kennedy and other politicians of the past, which were kept out of the respectable press). The rebellious acts of the not-so-distant past — living together before marriage, sleeping with someone you aren't going to marry, meeting someone at a party and going home with him — are now accepted as entirely normal. But they are not so acceptable that parents and teachers can teach them comfortably to teenagers. Without God, without rigid rules of social class, without reputations to worry about, we have no material out of which to form new values. We are left with a general feeling that someone has to tell these kids what to do about sex but no clear sense of what exactly it is that they should be told.

The haphazard way sex education works illustrates the breakdown of consensus: although seventeen states have mandates for sex education and thirty more support it, there is no standard curriculum, no basic texts that everyone reads, like *Hamlet* or *The Great Gatsby* in English classes. This relatively new and touchy subject is taught differently from state to state and classroom to classroom. Many teachers manage to avoid the words "sex" and "condoms," preferring to stick with the shadowy warning "Just be careful." The kids at a private school in Manhattan recall someone asking their science teacher how dangerous it was to give a blow job without a condom and his answering, "Just don't put yourself in that situation." The kids at Parsippany Hills recall their elementary-school sex education, which consisted of a gruff male gym teacher shouting, "What does it mean to jerk off?" at a group of blushing sixth-graders.

There is a surprising evasiveness behind all the candor: Pleasure is good. Masturbation is good. Teenage sex may or may not be good. The only certainty is in the microscopic germs clumped together on the black-and-white poster: *sleep around and you could wind up with more than a good time.* Parents and teachers think back through the dissolving years to their own youth, to going on the Pill, to the summer they found out that people of the opposite sex really wanted to sleep with them. Out of those pleasant sexual memories and present sexual fears, authority formulates itself cautiously: condoms are the only really tangible advice enlightened liberal adults have to offer. Pat Buchanan has put it this way: "Has America become a country where classroom discussion of the Ten Commandments is impermissible but teacher instructions on safe sodomy are to be mandatory?" In his high-blown rhetoric, he manages to capture a certain irony: in a time of shifting customs and evolving morals, condoms are the only absolute.

It's not that people aren't worried about "kids today." Every few months we seem to rediscover a crisis in teenage sexuality. The much-publicized release of the pseudodocumentary movie *Kids* in 1995 offered one such occasion, inspiring a *New York Times* headline that reads, " 'KIDS' EVOKES STRONG REACTIONS FROM YOUTHS AS WELL AS PARENTS." Critics called it a "wake-up call to the world"; they called it "shocking," "disturbing," "nihilistic," "gritty." As the movie drifts aimlessly along with its subjects through the various apartments, pools, and parks of New York City's teenage life, we get a pretty accurate picture of the urgency and impersonality of sixteen-year-old lust. The kids take what they want — money, sex, beer from a Korean grocery store — and the movie culminates in a party scene, with kids drinking and smoking and passing out everywhere in various stages of undress. One of the boys vomits into the toilet, and another has sex with a girl who has passed out on a leather couch. There is a Calvin Klein underwear ad element to the movie: it's a sultry world, where the kids slide up against each other like skateboards against pavement. You get the feeling that if you pulled one of these kids off the screen and asked her why she was behaving this way, she would shrug and say, "Why not?"

But the screenplay itself delivers a dramatic "why not": the AIDS virus. "Condoms suck," says one of the boys as they sit around doing whip-its and watching TV. Another says portentously to his friends, "That shit is made up. I don't know no one with AIDS." Of course one of them already has it, although he doesn't know it yet. A blond-haired, sweet-faced girl has it, too, even though she's slept with only one person. It is here that the "gritty realism" of the movie takes a conveniently moral turn. The movie tells these kids that this kind of behavior is wrong not because it's emotionally deadening or pointless, but because it may kill you. The reason not to have sex with a girl passed out at a party is that you might get a fatal virus. Two of the characters have it, and three more, including two trusting virgins, are exposed to it during the hour and a half we spend with them.

At the Angelika movie theater in Soho, pink flyers were pasted to the ticket booth saying, "KIDS is a movie about adolescent sexuality. . . . Some people may be offended. There will be no refunds. No one under 18 will be admitted unless accompanied by an adult." It's strange that this movie should seem so alarming, so anarchic and offensive to so many people, and that the screenwriter and filmmaker should be called "daring," when in fact the screenplay takes as its model something as banal and socially acceptable as the safe sex videos routinely shown to high school and college students. The plot faithfully follows the contours of countless educational videos and safe sex advertisements: someone believes that she won't get AIDS because she is practically a virgin and is not in any risk group; she has sex without a condom, and it turns out that she has been infected. The story of this "explosive" and "disturbing" movie has as clear a moral as a nineteenth-century classic like *Anna Karenina* or an eighteenth-century classic such as *Clarissa.* There is an almost poetic simplicity to the movie's message: illicit sexual acts lead to death.

Watching *Kids,* one can't help wondering where the adults are while all this drinking, pot smoking, and mindless sex is going on, which is something I remember wondering during my own teenage years. As Allan Bloom wrote in *The Closing of the American Mind,* "The constant newness of everything and the ceaseless moving from place to place, first radio, then television, have assaulted and overturned the privacy of the home. . . . Parents can no longer control the atmosphere of the home and have lost the will to do so." It may not be that parents have lost the *will* to control the atmosphere of their homes, but that since the sixties and seventies the certainty about what that control would ideally mean has broken down.

"My parents are just like, don't you dare," a pretty blond girl tells me. But many of the parents in Parsippany, like parents all over the country, don't feel entirely comfortable with the absoluteness of that kind of stance. Many of them seem to have no idea what to tell the strange creatures slamming doors and blaring music on the top floor of their homes. They don't want to be like Eisenhower era parents. They don't want their children to grow up "repressed," and they don't want them to get diseases. One nurse tells her seventeen-year-old son that, having lived through the social flux of the sixties and seventies and watched more and more of her friends' marriages end in divorce, she doesn't know what to tell him about his own life. This uncertainty, which many parents seem to share, most often results in the comic and awkward conversation known among these kids as "the condom talk," where the parent finally summons up the courage to tell the young teenager to use a condom and the young teenager says impatiently, "Oh, Mom, I know all about that stuff." This is another ritual that is not about what it appears to be about: the giving and receiving of information. Instead it operates as a kind of substitute tradition. It's an attempt to pass on some sort of wisdom and advice, the way mothers used to tell their daughters to stay virgins until they were married.

Given all the uncertainty about how sexual development is supposed to go, the institutional approach to the birds and the bees has its appeal. "I want her to learn about all of that in school," said a snowy-haired businessman I sat next to on a plane of his six-year-old daughter. "After everything I've done in my life, I frankly have no idea what I'd tell her."

One of the things that kids are learning in school is that what their parents tell them as they shift nervously on the couches of their own living rooms may be wrong. "My parents are so *ignorant* about sex," sighs a plump, freckled senior at Parsippany Hills High, and her complaint is echoed by a lot of kids there. Their parents may tell them that masturbation is bad or homosexuality immoral, but those are not acceptable attitudes — a point of view that is emphasized by a poster hanging in Room B-26 which says "Homosexuality, Heterosexuality, Bisexuality" in rainbow-colored stripes. The new open-minded, tolerant, technically up-to-date attitude about sex is going to come out of the classroom, not the home.

I confess that, sitting on an orange plastic chair in Room B-26 as the student teacher utters the words "Masturbation relieves tension," part of me is as repelled as the neatly groomed ladies in pale peach- and lemon-colored suits who don't want sex talked about in schools. I find myself wishing for a little reticence. I secretly sympathize with the sullen types — the boys and girls in black T-shirts, leather bands around their wrists, unwashed hair falling into their eyes — who find a little privacy in monosyllables, their minds wandering into reveries about Courtney Love or the sneakers they saw someone wearing yesterday at lunch. Anything but this. It seems to me that certain fantasies should remain untouched, that the X-rated movies playing in their minds belong to them. I have a kind of respect for these kids for not being drawn into the flat public confessions we are so fond of these days, for not giving in to the *Oprah*-like atmosphere of the classroom, for not wanting to talk about masturbation with their teachers.

I remember my own sex education. It took place one hot afternoon in seventh grade. It was 1980, the year these kids were born and years before AIDS lent its particular urgency to the whole venture. We had a science teacher named Mr. Tokieda, a small balding man who was supposed to answer our questions about sex. We were all girls, just on the verge of becoming sexual beings, and sort of drunk and unruly on the power we sensed that fact gave us over poor Mr. Tokieda. We were supposed to write our questions down and put them in a box, and he was supposed to answer them. We had a lot of questions, but we didn't ask them. Instead we made up extravagant questions, silly, obscene questions that would send a delicate pink blush across his face. I remember the hard teenage impulse well: *keep your real thoughts and feelings to yourself.* You can see this same sentiment in the penciled drawings in the margins of the Parsippany Hills kids' notebooks, in the drumming legs and fingers: the flight from discussion. There is a certain kind of knowledge that we have to grope our way toward on our own — on the vinyl seat of a car, after a few beers — certain questions that can't be answered multiple choice.

Although I wouldn't want to make an argument for fifties repression, nineties openness also seems, as one sits through a forty-minute class on masturbation, somewhat strange and unnatural. Sex, especially at that age, involves a fantasy of resistance, a fantasy of oneself and that other warm body against the world. It involves the illusion that this is the first time that anyone has ever done anything like this.

In the seventies a great deal of ink was spilt on the problem of repression. But the problem of repression may not, in fact, be worse than its opposite. Imagine Portnoy without a complaint. It's all laid out and demystified for him in junior high. Masturbation is only natural, Portnoy. It's the physical expression of yourself. It relieves tension and migraine headaches. The idea of creating a new kind of authority, a permissive, understanding authority, that appears in Technicolor and Dolby sound and encourages you to talk about your feelings, has its drawbacks, too. It creates the same painful sensation as when parents try to talk about Sonic Youth over breakfast. It leaves nothing to define yourself against. It leaves no space for Portnoy to be Portnoy.

The teacher standing in front of the blackboard says, "The safest form of sex is no sex." The kids stare blankly. The new morality being passed down to them is made of a flimsy material, of latex and *Oprah* and phrases like "communication" and "setting limits" and "self-esteem." If I were fifteen years old, I would run in the other direction. The problem is that for these kids, there is nowhere to run. They are supposed to conduct their personal lives in this undefined margin of doubt, in this climate of carefully cultivated and managed fear. It's no wonder, then, that the native, cliquish morality of teenage society takes on a new twist as they talk about a girl they all know. "She's done it with the whole school, and I know for a *fact* that she doesn't use condoms," explains one of the boys. "Man is she stupid," another one says, shaking his baseball-hatted head sadly. There is a general murmur of agreement on how stupid she is, coming most emphatically from the girls.

The tone of judgment and disapproval in their voices comes from nineties ideals of safety instead of fifties concerns about reputation, but it amounts to roughly the same thing. These kids are still looking down on the class slut for violating acceptable standards of behavior. Although the standards themselves have changed, the *need* for standards, for definitions of right and wrong, has not disappeared. If their parents felt guilty about sex — in the backseats of borrowed Fords and Chevrolets, and on front porches late at night, and in the fields behind their houses — these kids feel guilty about *risk*.

A boy who looks like a matinee idol from the fifties confesses in a smooth druggie drawl, "I got so hammered the other night that I passed out on the front steps of my house. My parents had to walk over me in the morning to get to work." After this standard display of teenage exhibitionism, he goes on to give a long, serious account of driving to another town to get an AIDS test with his girlfriend, his brother, and his brother's girlfriend, then waiting the next two weeks for the results. They just wanted to make sure. He'd done it a few times without a condom. It was the longest two weeks ever.

This jarring juxtaposition of recklessness and responsibility is what separates these teenagers from the ones who have come before: they are one part MTV and one part student health brochure. They talk about "hooking up" at parties and the difficulty of buying alcohol ("You know, it's easier for us to get weed than beer") and their late-night torments over whether they've gotten AIDS from each other. But what really surprises me is the absence of complaint, the familiar teenage cry of how unfair it all is. These kids seem to accept this state of affairs — where you get drunk out of your mind, pass out on the front steps of your parents' house, and go to get an AIDS test before having sex. It's the combination that bewilders: they are sexually sophisticated and childishly afraid.

O if thou hadst ever readmitted Adam into paradise,
how abstinently would he have walked by that tree.
— John Donne, 1626

Abstinence

"The true devout person breaks with nature to take pleasure in the abstinence of the pleasures," wrote Dryden in 1692. Three hundred years later, the sudden appearance of the word "abstinence" in newspapers, magazines, classrooms, and state legislatures marks a shift in our nation's moral life. Although it conjures up images of monks kneeling in monasteries and medieval saints fasting on rocks, abstinence now flits across our television screens as part of slick sex education efforts in which glowing young people proudly announce to us their desire not to have sex: "I can be . . . like a virgin." Former vice president Dan Quayle called it "the true cure" for AIDS, and Tommy Morrison, the HIV-infected boxer, has said that "the only real cure, the only 100 percent prevention for AIDS is abstinence." Abstinence, of course, is not a "cure" for AIDS. It is, however, the culmination of all the warnings in countless advertisements, brochures, and workshops about safer sex, date rape, and sexual harassment: it is caution in its purest, most condensed form.

A dark glass office building on L'Enfant Promenade in

downtown Washington, D.C., houses Concerned Women for America, the organization of conservative churchgoing women who were pushing abstinence long before it became fashionable. I suppose I went to their pink and powder blue offices in search of people who could say the word without irony. Concerned Women for America deplores everything that's happened since 1960: feminism, abortion rights, drugs, promiscuity, pornography, and violence in movies. It is also the kind of organization behind the flakier manifestations of the abstinence movement — videos with titles like *Wait for Me*, Christian rock songs like "Dare 2B Different" and "I Don't Want It," and the abstinence march in Washington, in which twenty thousand teenagers engaged in the bizarre symbolism of planting cards pledging their virginity into the soft earth of the nation's capital.

Concerned Women for America claims to have 600,000 paying members and chapters in all fifty states. Its founder, Beverly LaHaye, testifies before House and Senate committees and has just published a book on abstinence, *Against the Tide.*

"She's a gentle spirit," Beverly LaHaye's press secretary whispers to me as we walk down the long carpeted corridor, past the blond women in headbands and Ann Taylor suits rushing around the sleek office, typing, photocopying, and faxing their concern. Everyone who works here, explains the press secretary proudly, has signed a pledge of Christian faith. In spite of the imitation needlework platitudes about serving God hanging on the walls, this office, with its shelves lined with books, pamphlets, audiotapes, publicity folders, and videotapes, is anything but otherworldly. The building also contains a radio station, and at three o'clock in the afternoon Mrs. LaHaye's soothing bedtime-story voice goes out over the airwaves to three-quarters of a million Americans.

Outside Mrs. LaHaye's office two cute china angels are perched on the coffee table with a plaque explaining in loopy script, "Angels watching over you." As I sit next to the angels, Mrs. LaHaye's secretary leafs through five-by-seven glossies of her employer outfitted in the high Republican style of the mid-eighties: an optimistically bright red dress and a thick gold necklace. Mrs. LaHaye is also a pastor's wife, mother of four, and grandmother of nine, as her press kit eagerly tells us. The organization itself began as a group of women sitting around her kitchen table in southern California, drinking coffee, and chatting about declining morals in 1979.

Finally, Mrs. LaHaye herself ushers me into her office, which, with its pink ruffled drapes and oil painting of a single pink rose, seems more like somebody's grandmother's drawing room than the top of a glass office building in downtown Washington.

"Oh, dear," says Mrs. LaHaye. "What a day." Dressed in huge, dangling purple glass earrings, a matching purple dress, and bright pink lipstick, the founder of Concerned Women for America doesn't exactly look like a pastor's wife. When she talks, however, the phrases she uses seem to be lifted straight from an old-fashioned sermon: "Children must learn to be sexually pure until marriage," she says. I notice that the word "teenager" is conspicuously absent from her vocabulary: these nubile creatures pawing each other in the backseats of their parents' Chevrolets, she seems to suggest, are really just children.

Getting across the abstinence message hasn't been easy. Not only is Mrs. LaHaye battling the eternal forces of temptation, but she is also up against the schools — "their whole message is sex, sex, sex" — and "the entertainment industry."

With all of these forces against her, Beverly LaHaye has a powerful ally, the AIDS virus. Just as it has for more liberal sex educators, the virus has made Mrs. LaHaye's job as an abstinence evangelist easier. As moral and practical concerns seem to converge in the idea of chastity, AIDS has given the Christian Right a vivid reason for virtue where a more conventional moral argument has failed. In 1987 William Bennett, then secretary of education, and C. Everett Koop, then surgeon general, issued a joint statement on AIDS education: "Young people should be taught that the best precaution is abstinence until it is possible to establish a mutually faithful, monogamous relationship." It was mostly because of AIDS that abstinence — a proposition that seemed so repressive and outlandish at the end of the seventies — began to sound sensible to more and more people. The fear of God may not make anyone listen to Beverly LaHaye, with her pink lipstick and frosted hair, but the fear of AIDS will.

At the mention of the virus, Mrs. LaHaye's features arrange themselves into an expression of concern. "According to the teachings that I've had from God's Word," she says philosophically, "we pay a price for our actions." The "we" here is tactful, political, shrewd, because of course, as far as Mrs. LaHaye is concerned, *we* are not paying a price for our actions; *they* are. It's also her opinion that AIDS is inspiring older men to seek out high school virgins so that they won't be exposed to the disease. "It's the little girls who suffer," she says, shaking her head sadly, which is, of course, a strange statement to make about a disease that has primarily affected gay men.

But Beverly LaHaye is not Mother Teresa. She understands the ways of the world. "Parents shouldn't let sex be a no-no subject," she says, folding her hands and displaying her magnificently long pink nails. "It's something that was given to us by God to enjoy."

Mrs. LaHaye looks right past me into the clear blue skies and white painted houses of a vanished America. "When I was a child, my only pressure was whether or not I was going to win the spelling bee." She chuckles a deep grandmotherly chuckle. "We didn't learn about sex in school. We learned how to handle the family budget, how to shop wisely." Mrs. LaHaye has a slow, deliberate way of talking, perhaps hoping that if she talks slowly enough, the world might slow down with her.

"If you were raised on a farm," she continues, "you actually saw the cows procreating. Very normal. Very natural. You knew that when you got to that stage, you would procreate, too."

"You got to be a child then," says Mrs. LaHaye, her eyes still that heavenly blue. "Today's children aren't children. The worlds are as different as black from white."

For a moment her eyes dart toward the window, looking at the Washington Monument framed by heavy pink drapes, jutting into the sky.

"God bless you," she says as I leave, flashing me a radiant smile.

On the way out I see Beverly LaHaye's pretty press secretary bang her fist against the wall because she's just found out that another representative of the Christian Right is slotted to appear on *The MacNeil-Lehrer NewsHour*. "I've been on the phone with their people all week," she says, "and then they go and choose someone else."

Making my way to the elevator, I pass brass New England lanterns, too-shiny Chippendales, blond-wood-framed Colonial mirrors, and Revolutionary era tables. When I start looking closely, I realize that the entire office is furnished in imitation American antiques — cheap modern approximations of the past.

As I step out of the hushed air-conditioned office into the elevator, I can't wait to get out into the fresh, fallen world.

I end up going out to lunch with Beverly LaHaye's press secretary, Christine. From the outside Christine looks like any other twenty-six-year-old professional in Washington: long, neatly coiffed curls, round face, perfect smile, navy blue suit, beige stockings, and flat shoes. But she isn't. She doesn't live with her boyfriend who is a lawyer or a speechwriter or a congressional aide in a one-bedroom apartment on a winding street lined with pretty Victorian houses in Georgetown. She doesn't go out for gin and tonics with men she meets at parties. She is abstaining from sexual intercourse.

She is not a virgin, she tells me apologetically, as she picks up her turkey-and-avocado sandwich. She has what abstinence activists call "secondary virginity," which means that she has achieved her virginity through sheer force of will. This slightly less than perfect state of affairs came about because of the "promiscuous phase" she went through in college, when she "partied a lot" and skipped classes. That was before. Her light brown eyes flicker with a jittery contemplation of the past: the leather jackets, warm beer, alternative rock music, and sheets tangled on her dorm room floor. We look at each other in a moment of mutual understanding: *she is not as weird as I thought she was.*

"Don't you ever miss it?" I can't help asking.

"No," she says. I look skeptical. She looks beatific.

What's compelling about Christine is that she is not against sex, with her tinkling laugh and her insouciant smile; she is just saving it for marriage. "I was looking for love," she says of her past self. "That wasn't love." She has a point about whatever it is that happens between most seventeen-year-olds: "They're searching for something they'll never find in the physical act." Also probably true. There is a level of sophistication to Christine's unconventional choice. She is not like a schoolgirl in bobby socks who has never permitted herself to dream of warm naked bodies. She came to her decision after the same kind of experiences — flirting with friends, drinking at parties, waking up feeling awful — as almost everyone else.

True love waits, the slogan goes. But waiting for true love is not always easy. Christine is not just abstaining from sex; she is abstaining from a large part of the culture as well. She has defined herself against the movies people are talking about and the rock lyrics that get stuck in everyone else's head. She shuts it all out. Christine didn't go to see *Basic Instinct,* for instance, because even though she is "one hundred percent committed" to her beliefs, that kind of movie makes her feel, in her words, lonely. Not long ago a serious boyfriend broke up with Christine because of sex, or, as she puts it, "because he wanted to seek the world." Her voice trails off.

Sensing a moment of weakness, I search her face for signs of regret. There are none. Christine's faith in the future is unlimited. She has turned her back on a world of divorce and affairs, sudden flashes of desire, instant passion, thrilling sensations, and the whole precarious and anarchic pursuit of pleasure. In its place she has something else: a sublime confidence in her reward. "God hasn't yet given me that special guy," she says, mixing King James with *Cosmopolitan*, but she is certain that he will. She is also certain that when he does, she and that special guy will live happily ever after. "Love is patient," says Christine, quoting 1 Corinthians as she takes a large bite of her "California Sandwich." I observe that this isn't true of any of the love that I have ever experienced, and Christine laughs her tinkling laugh.

People who aren't religious should be abstinent, too, she explains. It's the only way to protect yourself from disease. I mention the possibility of using condoms, and Christine looks at me, appalled, as though I have just suggested that you can't get pregnant the first time. "Condoms *break*," she says. She explains patiently that the pores in latex are big enough for the AIDS virus to get through. "It's like trying to stop water with a chain-link fence." While I contemplate this dubious scientific fact, she goes on to denounce "the myth of safe sex," which, with its juicy conspiratorial feel, is a favorite phrase among abstinence activists.

The alchemy of wishful thinking and moral judgment magically creates its own facts: birth control fails; condoms don't protect you from disease. I've always heard that condoms, used correctly, are 99 percent effective. The pores in expensive animal skin condoms may be too large to prevent disease, but not in the far more common latex variety. It would seem pretty hard to get around these widely accepted truths, but Christine argues hotly for a physical universe in which sexually transmitted diseases can never be avoided by the sexually active. She seems convinced that condoms themselves are fabricated out of the dreams and fantasies of sinners. The barely submerged suggestion is that the liberal media and the condom companies and the sex educators, who know that condoms don't work and continue to push them anyway, are deliberately killing our children.

And behind her false science is the real fear that's mirrored in the larger culture: sex is never safe. Its dangers go beyond the prosaic realities of pregnancy and disease into the bright secrets of the soul. Several years ago Christine went back to her old high school in the affluent suburb of Morristown, New Jersey, to deliver a talk on the power of abstinence. She met a seventeen-year-old, "a really beautiful girl," who had slept with thirty men. This seventeen-year-old Mary Magdalene tried to change, but it was too late. After losing all her "self-esteem," she slipped into a life of drugs and prostitution. As Christine tells the story, her caramel-colored eyes fill with the kind of relieved concern that people safely inside during a rainstorm feel as they watch the pedestrians struggling against the torrents. Through the glass panes, she is seeing her phantom self: some other possible course her life could have taken.

One of the most powerful premises of the Christian Right is that "sin begets sin." Sex itself is such a powerful, uncontrollable force that once you give in to it, you get swept into a whirlpool of desire. The seventeen-year-old winner of Concerned Women for America's abstinence college scholarship,

John, announced in a radio broadcast, "Once a person gratifies their desire, it increases. Pretty soon they go on a rampage." The belief that if you start having sex, you'll never be able to restrain yourself is embedded deeply enough in the American psyche that the idea seems almost natural to us; it plays on our fundamentally puritanical distrust of pleasure. It's all or nothing. It's abstinence or prostitution. The imaginative power of these extremes lends credence to the abstinence movement: self-control is so absolutely necessary because the loud music of excess is so tempting, so seductive, and so near.

I have to admit that Christine does have a certain glow. It resembles happiness but may in fact be something more like delusion. She is living in another America, one where you talk about God's will and honoring your parents, where your father brings a freshly cut Christmas tree into the house and Santa Claus tumbles merrily down the chimney. It's a world one thinks of as mostly inhabited by old people, which is why it's jarring to hear a pretty, articulate twenty-six-year-old espousing the doctrine of sexual purity. I find myself infuriated. I suddenly want to convert her more desperately than she wants to convert me, although there are definitely times when I wish that, like Christine, I had a giant book that would tell me how to live my life instead of a copy of *Elle* to tell me how to kiss, *Anna Karenina* to tell me not to cheat on my husband, and a John Updike paperback to tell me how to go about it if I do. At the hairdresser's I pick up a copy of *Harper's Bazaar*, which has the words "Adultery: Can Cheating Help a Marriage?" printed next to the luminous blond head of the cover model. There is no transcendent wisdom; there are only stories. And it's easy to feel, amidst all the tolerant, glossy fragments of advice, a great drive toward the stern old-fashioned morality that would pull it all together.

Although Christine is sitting right across the table, across half-empty plates and crumpled napkins, it suddenly seems like there is a vast distance between us. It's the distance between "Adultery: Can Cheating Help a Marriage?" and "Thou shalt not commit adultery," between fluttering psychological questions ("What would make me happy?" "What would be the healthy thing to do?") and moral certainty. Christine doesn't spend hours on the phone with her friends talking about what she should do about her ex-boyfriend and whether she should have a fling with a man from her office. "I'm just waiting for the right person," she says calmly. I don't say anything calmly.

Christine turns to the waitress and asks, "Can I have a decaffeinated coffee with whipped cream?" and when the waitress delivers the large china cup of unreal coffee with its childish white puff of cream on top, I think to myself, *That figures.*

"Abstinence" is a neutral word with a clean, scientific ring. The absolutism of its message notwithstanding, it's primarily practical rather than fanatical, bureaucratic rather than religious. The word arose out of a gradual disenchantment with the sexual permissiveness of the sixties and seventies. The frequency with which it's been cropping up signals a reaction against the images of sexually sophisticated teenagers that fills jeans ads, women's magazines, and television shows. But the cultural conversation about abstinence is not just about teenagers and whether or not we think fifteen-year-olds should sleep around;

it's also a reflection of what the rest of us are thinking about ourselves. We look at the messiness of our own lives — divorces, affairs, stepchildren, broken homes — and the future messiness contained in that blank, defiant teenage expression *I'll do whatever I want,* and we contemplate with relief the prospect of a strong moral code, a strictly ordered life. Thou shalt not.

Abstinence is an old tradition in a glossy new package: it comes at us as revelation. Teenagers don't *have* to have sex. The increased casualness with which we talk about abstinence allows for a critique of hedonism that has so far been reserved for the William Bennetts and Bob Doles of the world. Miss South Carolina rhapsodized about it at the 1995 Miss America Pageant. And even President Bill Clinton, the overweight, virile symbol of a certain kind of liberalism, has, in his throaty voice, expounded on the virtues of abstinence for young people — a sign, perhaps, that the sixties themselves have finally given in. The word itself embodies a strong, straightforward stance toward sexuality that we don't really have.

"No petting if you want to be free," commands "Sex Respect," the first, largest, and most radical of the new abstinence curricula that are circulating through the country. Partially funded by the Reagan administration and actually taught in more than 10 percent of the school districts around the country, "Sex Respect" is an unapologetic effort at indoctrination. The program was designed by Coleen Kelly Mast, whose name — along with her beaming face on the back cover — suggests that she was voted homecoming queen or most likely to succeed. The strange pages of "Sex Respect" are illustrated with cartoon teenagers who seem, in spite of the

"New! Revised for the Nineties" label optimistically attached to the front cover, to have stepped out of another decade. In ill-fitting jeans, long-sleeved button-down shirts, and midcalf-length skirts, they're dressed in the style of unpopular teenagers from the fifties, and they speak in a faded vernacular about "necking" and being "square." To sell the idea of chastity, Mast has come up with darkly cute aphorisms such as "Pet your dog, not your date"; "Control your urgin', be a virgin"; "Don't be a louse, wait for your spouse"; "Do the right thing, wait for the ring"; "Keep ALL of your clothes on, ALL of the way, ALL of the time. AVOID AROUSAL."

Coleen Kelly Mast is right that abstinence is a hard sell. I recall my sophomore year of college, when a friend leaned over her green plastic tray in the dining hall and whispered contemptuously about another girl, "She's a *virgin*." I strained to get a glimpse of this perfectly normal-looking girl who was eating her pale green cafeteria salad several tables away, as if there were something terribly wrong with her. Being free from the rigid values of social convention no longer means going home with a man you meet in a bar or hiding birth control pills in the cotton depths of your underwear drawer. In resisting the pressure to be carefree and defying the seductive authority of their peers, the virgin eating her salad and the Christines of the world are, in the end, our true rebels. It's not hard to imagine, through the dissolving years, the ideal audience for the abstinence message: the anxious teenager who has no idea which kind of jeans to buy, who hasn't been asked out and maybe never will, who catches a fleeting reflection of herself in the mirror and thinks that she is too fat or too thin. In other words almost all of them. The abstinence movement artfully plays on the deepest fears and insecurities of adolescence with the tempting offer that you don't really have to grow up.

A pretty image of childhood emerges from the abstinence propaganda in which children spontaneously go caroling "any time of year," drink pineapple floats, and make pizzas together. These are the activities that "Sex Respect" suggests instead of jumping into bed together. The abstinence movement is trying to obliterate the idea of adolescence, and in this effort lies its appeal. There may not have been a single pineapple float consumed in America for forty years, but out of these gentle suggestions comes the reassuring vision that we are still particularly susceptible to, in which twelve-year-old girls play with soft stuffed animals instead of trying on tight vinyl miniskirts at the mall. If the idea of abstinence is filling some deep social need, it is precisely this longing for innocence on the part of sixteen-year-olds themselves and the culture as a whole. It is holding out the promise that if we answer the multiple-choice questions and keep all of our clothes on all of the time, we can make ourselves virtuous again.

In its journey from the sanctuaries of the Christian Right to the blackboards of public schools, the word "abstinence" has been cleansed of all traces of Beverly LaHaye. Even in the doctrinaire pages of "Sex Respect," the underlying religious message has been cleverly erased. Its students are taught how not to have sex in excruciating detail, but they are not really taught *why*. You can feel the curriculum desperately searching for a raison d'être as it assembles a random collection of practical justifications: AIDS and pregnancy (since the cartoon teenagers are, like Christine, living in a world where condoms and other forms of birth control don't work); pop psychological platitudes about "healthy sexuality," "self-esteem," and "fulfillment"; and the more creative proposition that abstinence enhances sexual satisfaction within marriage. What's missing is the ideological force that pulls it all together: *God says premarital sex is wrong.*

This forced casualness is partly a product of the separation of church and state and what it's legal to say in front of classrooms filled with public school children, but the abstinence movement is also responding to a strange and definite need: we seem to want the forms of religion without the content. To tailor such a program, the abstinence movement has to stretch the facts: French-kissing causes AIDS in the pages of "Sex Respect" because there *needs* to be a reason why it's wrong.

Outspoken proponents of a "culture of abstinence" are not confined to the Christian Right. "Heroic individual self-denial is not a viable long term adolescent policy," wrote Lance Morrow in *Time*. "What might work, however, would be an entire context of abstinence, a culture of abstinence." He went on to say that having sex will help the teenager find his "work" and sense of purpose. In the pages of "Sex Respect," abstinence will help him learn to communicate with the opposite sex and concentrate on the future. The visionaries of the abstinence movement seem to think that abstaining from sexual intercourse will save the teenager not just from disease but also from confusion, heartbreak, jealousy, and pain. But this is as utopian, and ultimately unrealistic, as the opposite point of view that emerged in the seventies: that young people would be saved by sexual freedom and openness.

The real problem with the abstinence movement is that it

isn't a radical rethinking of the sexual revolution. It still puts sex in a majestic position in the center of life. It infuses the minutiae of the physical act — the yes or no, and how far and with whom, and which pieces of clothes end up in a tangled heap on the floor — with a puritanical importance.

It's hard to imagine what the broader appeal of a "culture of abstinence" could possibly be, but there is something in the idea that has begun to seem reasonable. It's not just the concern about teenage pregnancy and AIDS but a deeper wish for clarity, an imaginary solution to some of the more complicated problems posed by the sexual freedom we've inherited from the sixties and seventies. But what could be wrong with freedom? It's not the absence of rules exactly, the dizzying sense that we can do whatever we want, but the sudden realization that nothing we do matters. The decision to sleep with someone, which feels so pressing, so momentous, so absolutely crucial, means nothing. It will vanish into the spin cycle of the washing machine with the sheets. *Can cheating help a marriage?* Maybe, maybe not. But it's this gentle moral relativism, combined with the lack of consequences, with legal abortion and easy-to-obtain birth control, that brings out our vestigial need for strong social codes, for judgment, context, and tradition, for a sense that whatever happens has some meaning outside our own bedrooms.

I remember being up late one night drinking red wine with a man whom I wasn't really supposed to be seeing. This was not someone I was in a relationship with. It was not someone who, in the strictest terms of the fifties propriety that we still tenuously hold on to, I should have been with at all. But the decision was made. I ended up staying the night. When I woke up — the red alarm clock flashing 7:00 A.M., light pouring in, the unshaven man still sleeping next to me, wrapped in his boyish striped sheets — I crept out of the apartment, in my clothes from the night before, rumpled, hair tangled, worrying as I passed the bald doorman that he would look at me in the bright fluorescence of the lobby and know. But he barely glanced up from his coffee regular and *New York Post* sports scores to register my presence. I walked quickly out into the cold morning, still thinking that the men and women rushing past in their camel hair coats — neatly combed, freshly washed hair, newspapers tucked under their arms — would notice, but, of course, they just rushed past. And it came to me, with a surprising rush of disappointment, that no one cared. And even if they had known, they still wouldn't have cared.

Disappointment was, of course, an odd response. You'd think I would have been able to enjoy the general permissiveness that allowed the doorman to go on reading his sports scores as I stumbled past him. But the ease with which we can now slip in and out of intimacy, the sheer convenience of it, is not as desirable as it might once have seemed. Think of the high romance of *Anna Karenina* and how dependent it is on the outrage of the outside world. When Anna and Vronsky fall into bed together for the first time, they have an excruciating realization that their whole world has, after that one fleeting physical act, changed forever: "She would have fallen on the carpet if he had not held her. 'Oh god, forgive me,' she said, sobbing and pressing his hands to her breast. She felt so sinful, so guilty that nothing was left to her but to humble herself and beg forgiveness; but she had no one in the world now but him."

Amidst her sobbing, Anna knows, in exquisite detail, the moral and social meaning of her act. She will never again be received in her elegant black velvet gown into the homes of her friends. She will never be able to go to the theater without being frowned upon by society. She won't even be able to visit her son. Life as she has known it is over. The painful consequences of her affair give it a beauty and a meaning beyond the physical act itself. It is the consequences that lift her affair out of the ordinariness of carnality and the mutability of feeling and give it its eternal romantic meaning: *here is what defines love.*

We find ourselves living without the pain, reassurance, and clarity of late-nineteenth-century social censure. We are on our own. Although there are obvious drawbacks to the situation in which Anna Karenina finds herself — the prejudice, the snobbery, the scorn, the sexism, the fact that she ultimately has to hurl herself under a train — we still find ourselves yearning for consequences. Meaning. A tiny ruffling of the social order. If an act has serious social ramifications, like Anna's affair with Vronsky, then it appears to have transcendent meaning as well. It matters. It changes things. Anna's whole experience of her affair — the sobbing, the guilt, the trembling — come in part from the knowledge of how it will reverberate in the world outside Vronsky's bedroom. It is the reaction of society that gives the affair its outline and definition and engraves it indelibly into their lives.

A century later, these sorts of things are easily erased: a diaphragm put back into the medicine cabinet, friends chattily confided in over lunch, a divorce lawyer hired after a few phone calls. Today's Anna Karenina would sit with her psychiatrist calmly talking about whether cheating might save her marriage, whether or not she should tell her husband, and what it is about his character that led her to do it in the first place. And as she sits in the psychiatrist's book-lined, plant-filled office sorting through the exquisite agonies of her affair, there would be some small part of her that secretly longs for the baroque grandeur of nineteenth-century scandal.

The end of consequences has created a new moral universe in which events such as Anna Karenina's adulterous affair can seem formless and weightless. Gone are the days when illicit couples had to register in hotel rooms under the name "Mr. and Mrs. John Smith." As they ride up the elevator to the sinful anonymity of their double suite with minibar and color TV, "Mr. and Mrs. John Smith" are now left with the naked solitude of their real names: the unsettling knowledge that they are *not* playing a role in any larger social drama. And along with the freedom this new tolerance allows comes a certain sense of pointlessness. This may be what Allan Bloom meant when he wrote in *The Closing of the American Mind* that "passionlessness is the most striking effect, or revelation, of the sexual revolution."

That sense of depressing futility — that it's just us and our physical desires, that cheating *can* help a marriage, that all that matters is what's fun or psychologically healthy — is what gives an idea such as abstinence its appeal. Our ecstatic individualism, which is as close as present-day America comes to having religion, urges us: *Please yourself. Express yourself. Fulfill yourself.* The moral codes of the past gave us a kind of definition: "I am Anna Karenina in opposition to the petty bourgeois morality of my day." But without the petty bourgeois morality, the tragic proportions of Anna's affair diminish into mundane practical concerns such as where to meet and how long the excitement will last and which one of her friends to tell.

And this is precisely what a "culture of abstinence," in its forced, awkward way, appears to be offering. Who you fall into bed with is not simply a question of personal happiness or psychological health. The abstinence movement promises an escape from the nihilistic situation in which people have sex or don't have sex and wake up the next day and drink coffee out of Styrofoam cups, as the world looks on, in the pale light of morning, with absolute indifference. It adds a bright gloss of moral significance to the most intimate choices: *what you're doing matters.*

It's precisely the nostalgic appeal of abstinence — and sexual harassment codes, date-rape pamphlets, "safer sex," and books like *The Rules* — that draws us in, the unwillingness to indulge the psychological complexities, ambiguities, motivations, and desires of the individual; in short, the unwillingness to say *Do whatever makes you feel good.* Here, finally, are rules to live by. They are charged with the energy of politics and safety. They take away the terror and responsibility that two decades of relative sexual freedom seem to have left us with: we don't have to create our own meaning. But abstinence, ripped out of its religious context, has no more substance than any other commercial jingle. "Do the right thing, wait for the ring" makes no more sense than "Coke is it!" It gives us a code of conduct without a reason to follow it. Abstinence isn't moral certainty. It's an unsatisfying substitute. It's a kind of morality light.

Abstinence, sexual harassment codes, date-rape pamphlets,

"safer sex," and *The Rules* give us the fervor, the romance and trappings, of self-denial without its deeper moral purpose. There is something sad about the wholesome-looking teenagers in television advertisements saying, "I'm saving myself until marriage" or "I've realized I can be . . . like a virgin," and that is how much we long for moral clarity and how impossible it is for us to have it. We are caught in the paradoxes of our own excesses. We live with both the sexual revolution and the reaction *against* the sexual revolution. We struggle with the desire to be wild and not wild, to be careful and not careful, to be free and not free, to do whatever we feel like after two drinks on a Saturday night, and to be bound by the rules; and it's in the uneasiness and confusion of this struggle that most of us love and are loved.

Acknowledgments

I am indebted to everyone who gave me their time and thoughts during the research of this book, especially the students I talked to at Parsippany Hills High School, Brearley, Dalton, Stuyvesant High School, Vanderbilt, Tulane, Shoreline Community College, the University of Washington at Seattle, the University of Utah, Harvard, Brown, and Princeton; and to Susan Wilson from the New Jersey Network for Family Life Education, Vic Zeigel from the *Daily News,* Carole Adamsbaum, Robin Murphy, Lydia Ogden from the Centers for Disease Control, Dr. Gerald Friedland, Larry Kramer, Christopher Foreman, Ethan Gutmann, Adam Glickman, Katherine Pope, and Joan Gardiner.

I owe thanks to Jim Silberman and Alexandra Pringle for their advice and encouragement; and thanks also to Becky Michaels and Marsinay Smith.

I am more grateful than I can express to my friends, especially Richard Lamb, David Lipsky, Larissa Macfarquhar, Ben Metcalf, Inigo Thomas, Daniel Max, and David Bennahum; to my family, Anne and Herman Roiphe, Becky, Emily, Bruce, Jean, Michael, and Marco; and to Suzanne Gluck, Jordan Pavlin, and Catherine Crawford.